ART & DESIGN

D1706331

EDITORIAL OFFICES:
42 LEINSTER GARDENS, LONDON W2 3AN
TEL: 071-402 2141 FAX: 071-723 9540

HOUSE EDITOR: Nicola Hodges;
EDITORIAL: Katherine MacInnes;
SENIOR DESIGNER: Andrea Bettella;
DESIGN CO-ORDINATOR: Mario Bettella;
DESIGN TEAM: Meret Gabra-Liddell
Jason Rigby

SUBSCRIPTION OFFICES:
UK: VCH PUBLISHERS (UK) LTD
8 WELLINGTON COURT, WELLINGTON STREET
CAMBRIDGE CB1 1HZ   UK

USA: VCH PUBLISHERS INC
303 NW 12TH AVENUE DEERFIELD BEECH,
FLORIDA 33442-1788 USA

ALL OTHER COUNTRIES:
VCH VERLAGSGESELLSCHAFT MBH
BOSCHSTRASSE 12, POSTFACH 101161
69451 WEINHEIM   GERMANY

© 1994 *Academy Group Ltd*. All rights reserved. No part of this publication may be reproduced or transmitted in any form or by any means, electronic or mechanical, including photocopying, recording or any information storage or retrieval system without permission in writing from the Publishers. Neither the Editor nor the Academy Group hold themselves responsible for the opinions expressed by writers of articles or letters in this magazine. The Editor will give careful consideration to unsolicited articles, photographs and drawings; please enclose a stamped addressed envelope for their return (if required). Payment for material appearing in *A&D* is not normally made except by prior arrangement. All reasonable care will be taken of material in the possession of *A&D* and agents and printers, but they regret that they cannot be held responsible for any loss or damage.
 Art & Design is published six times per year (Jan/ Feb; Mar/Apr; May/Jun; Jul/Aug; Sept/Oct; and Nov/ Dec). Subscription rates for 1994 (incl p&p): *Annual subscription price*: UK only £65.00, World DM 195, USA $135.00 for regular subscribers. *Student rate*: UK only £50.00, World DM 156, USA $105.00 incl postage and handling charges. *Individual issues*: £14.95/DM 39.50 (plus £2.30/DM 5 for p&p, per issue ordered), US$24.95 (incl p&p).
 For the USA and Canada, *Art & Design* is distributed by VCH Publishers, Inc, 303 NW 12th Avenue, Deerfield Beach, FL 33442-1788; Telefax (305) 428-8201; Telephone (305) 428-5566 or (800) 367-8249. Application to mail at second-class postage rates is pending at Deerfield Beach, FL Postmaster: Send address changes to *Art & Design*, 303 NW 12th Avenue, Deerfield Beach, FL 33442-1788.Repro by Print Tek London.Printed in Italy. All prices are subject to change without notice. [ISSN: 0267-3991]

CONTENTS

ART & DESIGN **MAGAZINE**

ART & DESIGN **PROFILE** No 35

NEW ART FROM EASTERN EUROPE
Identity and Conflict

Mirosław Bałka, '367x241x25', 1993

Ilya Kabakov, The Red Pavilion, 1993 (Ronald Feldman Fine Arts, New York, photo Norbert Artner)

'Hollywood' · redesigned by Trio · Sarajevo

Hollywood on Trebvić, redesigned by TRIO, Sarajevo, 1993

II

EUROPE WITHOUT WALLS

ART, POSTERS AND REVOLUTION

Ever since the Berlin Wall came down, we have seen countless images of life in what was the Eastern bloc – images chosen for underlining what we in the West are not.

An exhibition at Manchester City Art Galleries (13 November 1993 –16 January 1994) brought together over 100 artworks from the Czech Republic, East Germany, Hungary, Poland, Russia and elsewhere, piecing together a different view of these turbulent years.

Many of these, and more, have been published in a book brought out by the co-curators to accompany the exhibition. Images include crude street graffiti, satirical cartoons featuring bananas (consumerism) and cabbages (German-ness), and raw documentary photography overprinted with cris de coeur (*Lithuania be Free*, 1991).

There are also traditional oil paintings, and more knowingly conceptual work, such as that by the Czech Milan Knížák, or the 'actions' by the collective the Neo-Stunners, who work in Duchampian mode and whose *Pink Tank* in Prague hit the popular consciousness worldwide. Recurrent images are of the dead Christ and of idealised youths; hares, too, abound, most famously those painted by Manfred Butzmann in November 1989 on the east side of the Berlin Wall itself; symbols of the only occupants of the dead zone, they also have an eye to the ecology movement and to Joseph Beuys as well.

There are other artistic references, with famous paintings doctored to polemic effect: Caspar David Friedrich's romantic wanderers gaze out over scenes of ecological disaster in works by the East German, Joseph Huber; *Flora*, by Russian N Zhuravleva, depicts the familiar Botticelli figure against the background of a destroyed forest;

Mantegna's dead Christ is assaulted by Russian typography, literally pierced by a red wedge in *Beat the Whites with the Red Wedge* by Andrei Kolosov and Valeria Kovigina (1990).

Most of the works are in the form of handbills, postcards and posters – the media of reform, intended for a mass audience. (Two curators – one from Brno, the other from the Victoria and Albert Museum in London – had the foresight to tear down the posters for posterity.) The forum for debate is the street, and the relationship between art and life is very different from that in the West. This is put into context in the opening essay by James Aulich, who sees the idea of decoding fictions, of reading between the lines, as fundamental to those living in a police state, making art not an elite taste but an essential, non-lethal weapon.

Matthias Flügge looks at this same issue in the context of the former GDR, asking whether art could be credited with having paved the way for change. Baselitz, who left East Germany in the 50s, maintained that any artist who cared about freedom would have followed him.

Other art historians and art critics from the East offer further insights; but perhaps the most chastening (and entertaining) piece is Gregory McLaughlin's closing account of how British television and newspaper reporting of the revolutions of 1989, couched as they are in the language of consumerism, reveals far more about how the West views itself than it ever could about life in the former Eastern bloc.

EUROPE WITHOUT WALLS Art, Posters and Revolution 1989-93, *exhibition catalogue, edited by James Aulich and Tim Wilcox, Manchester City Art Galleries, 208pp, HB £25.95 PB £16.95*

L TO R: David Černý and the Neo-Stunners, The Pink Tank, *1991; Klaus Staeck,* Brandenburger Tor Rückseite (Brandenburg Gate, Rear View), *1990; OPPOSITE: Wolf Vostell,* Wer ohne Sunde ist ('He that is without sin . . .', *1990; OVERLEAF BACKGROUND: Students of the Academy of Applied Arts & Science, Prague,* 100 Czech Crowns, *1989; L TO R: Holger Fickelscherer,* Alles Banane (It's all Bananas), *1989; Manfred Butzmann,* Green! Red!, *1991; Andrei Kolosov and Valeria Kovrigina,* Beat the Whites with the Red Wedge, *1990*

UNWANTED MONUMENTS OF WARSAW

Halina Taborska

During 1919, in towns and villages of the newly formed Soviet Union, a poster appeared representing a rearing bronze horse over a fallen male figure, and a classical temple, amid scattered illuminated manuscripts, with huge letters demanding in the imperative manner of propagandist slogans of the day: 'Citizens, protect monuments of art'. The campaign had the blessing of Lenin, who decided in the early days of the Revolution to give some protection to the cultural heritage of Russia's Tsarist past. Nobody today seems to be willing to protect Lenin; his painted images, busts, reliefs and statues tumble down to the applause of free people from the East and the West, and it serves him right, they say. In any case, the comparison with the post-October situation does not hold. The monuments of Tsarist Russia came into existence through the will and beliefs of people who, even if perceived as an oppressive ruling class, did represent the culture, aspirations and artistic ability of their nation. This cannot be said about the monuments imposed on the peoples of Eastern Europe through the will or whim of a foreign power and the regimes kept in place by the coercion of hidden or overt military threat.

Warsaw had no impressive Lenin or Stalin statues to dispose of, but it did have the next best thing. Felix Dzierzynski, founder of Russia's notorious Secret Police and the People's Commissar for Internal Affairs, whose Polish origins made him particularly dear to Polish communists, was known to the Warsaw populace as 'Felix, bloody little hand', and referred to as 'the one who loved children, but hated their parents'. His huge monument was erected in July 1951 in one of the most prominent locations of Warsaw, the 'Bankowy' Square, henceforth renamed Dzierzynski Square. Sculpted by Zbigniew Dunajewski, in the style of romanticised Socialist Realism, it had as its back-drop a remarkable group of three classicist mansions designed in the 1820s for the Treasury Department by an Italian architect, Antonio Corazzi. Against a spectacular row of Doric and Ionic porticos and arcades, in one of the busiest thoroughfares of the city, Dzierzynski rose high on a granite pedestal, within sight of Warsaw's dreaded Security and Militia Headquarters, housed in the former Potocki Palace. He fell on 16 November 1989 in a manner worthy of a Sergei Eisenstein film. His huge body, made of concrete with bronze coating, in a noose of thick rope, was jerked from its pedestal, hovered briefly in the air, broke into three massive chunks, lost its head and crashed to the ground amid the applause of the watching crowd, allegedly never to rise again. However, and here the analogy with Eisenstein's *October* works well, Felix rose from the rubble briefly in 1992, when the amazed and somewhat shaken Warsovians saw his distinct figure looking 'as if alive' against the morning sky. It was reconstructed as a maquette for a short film by Krzysztof Magowski entitled 'Felix Dzierzynski Lands in Warsaw', about a fictitious coup, which brings back the old communist regime which sees as first on its list of priorities the rebuilding of the Dzierzynski monument. The hero of the film's title, the great-grandson and namesake of Felix, arrives in Warsaw to participate in the unveiling of the monument. In fact, the removal of the Dzierzynski statue caused serious embarrassment to the first Prime Minister of the new Poland, Tadeusz Mazowiecki, who visited Moscow shortly after the event, and heard Soviet officials complaining bitterly about the deposition of the great hero of the October Revolution.

Felix's prominent siting was matched by the truly provocative positioning of a much bigger, but equally hated monument 'To those who fell defending the Polish People's Republic'. On the so-called 'Saski' (Saxon) axis, which opens with the 'Tomb of the Unknown Soldier', runs along the central avenue of the oldest public garden in Warsaw, the 'Saski' Garden, and terminates with the distant view of the Lubomirski Palace, a piazza was paved with marble slabs to support an enormous multi-figure monument made of bronze and stone. The site was designated in 1952 for a never-erected statue of Joseph Stalin, then in the 1960s for an abandoned Victory-arch; finally, in 1985, General Jaruzelski unveiled there the 'eternal' memorial which was destined for a very short life. It was conceived in the days of military rule, by the Ministry of the Interior, designed by a Professor of the Warsaw Academy of Fine Arts, Bohdan Chmielewski, and was dedicated to those who died as builders, defenders and martyrs of communist Poland. It was exceptionally hideous, with figures

Successive stages of the deposition of the statue of Felix Dzierzynski, 1989

in histrionic poses pointing towards and supporting with their outstretched arms a crownless Polish eagle, while others stared into space with mournful steadfastness. The monument completely obscured the facade of the Palace, ruined the vista of the Saxon axis and was perceived by the people of Warsaw as an act of political provocation. On 29 July 1991, the Warsaw Council decided to dismantle it, and five workers from the same Gliwice foundry which had made and erected the monument, cut and unscrewed it into several smaller elements. The official reason given for its removal was that it had been built without the permission of the City's planning authorities.

Such an excuse cannot be provided for the removal of one of the oldest large Socialist Realist monuments in Warsaw, which commemorates the soldiers of the Red Army. It was constructed in 1945, inscribed 'Glory to the heroes of the Soviet Army' and dedicated to 'Comrades in arms who gave their lives for the freedom and independence of the Polish nation'. The monument was allegedly erected by the 'inhabitants of Warsaw'.

Since it was the Red Army which brought to the city of Warsaw, devastated by war and years of German occupation, 45 years of uninvited communist rule, many of its citizens object to the presence of this memorial in a very busy street of Praga, a residential and commercial district, on the east bank of the Vistula River. Unfortunately, the huge structure, made of red granite and grey stone, looks as solid as the Pyramids. On its four sides, wide steps flank a tall pedestal, crowned with a bronze group of three soldiers in combat postures. Armed with submachine guns and a hand-grenade, they charge westwards. This is not a bad group of its kind, as it does convey a sense of desperate urgency, an almost suicidal determination which drove the soldiers of the Red Army forward in their final race to capture Berlin. Near to the ground at the four corners stand the soldiers in military coats with weapons close to their bodies, heads bent, immobile and solemn, which earned the monument its nickname, 'The Four Sleepers'. Two of the four represent the First Polish Army formed in the Soviet Union under the command of General Berling, which fought alongside the Reds on the Eastern Front, and participated in the capture of Berlin, hence another official name given to the monument, 'To Brotherhood in Arms'. One of the highly emotive and fatal turning-points in the complex history of 20th-century Poland came when the Soviet allies and comrades in armed struggle became, by the same token, oppressors and bearers of the hated communist regime. So, the Poles asked, what should be done with such monuments?

There is the often costly alternative of careful dismantling and storage, or establishing museums and open air sculpture parks for the disgraced symbols. One well known museum of Socialist Realist art already exists in Poland, but it houses

mainly paintings and smaller pieces of sculpture. The collection consists of approximately 1,500 items and was formed in the years 1960-70, when the Ministry of Culture and Art sent its unwanted works for storage in a Palace-Museum of the Zamoyski family in Kozlowka. Now some of the exhibits, including 40 pieces of sculpture, are shown in an exhibition called 'Stalin's Breath', presenting works from the short period of 'pure' Socialist Realism in Poland, which lasted from 1949 to 1955. A larger permanent display is planned for 1994 in a renovated former coach house of the Palace. Of the gigantic discarded monuments, only one, brought here from the nearby town of Lublin, stands discretely hidden among the tall trees of the Palace park. It represents the first communist president and the General Secretary of the Polish Workers Party, Boleslaw Bierut.

In Cracow, a major project is under discussion, a 'scansen park' of the Polish People's Republic, showing 45 years of its existence, through its deposed monuments, old soc-realist films and newsreels, with a library of Marxist classics and an old style restaurant offering a herring and dill cucumber menu. It will be serviced by young attendants in red ties and clothes once worn by members of the 'Union of Polish Youth'. The considered location is in Nowa Huta, an industrial town near Cracow, established in the early 1950s for the labour force of the vast 'Lenin' steelworks. Unfortunately, the park could not contain a once famous and often attacked Nowa Huta 'Lenin' sculpture, as it was dismantled in early 1990 and sold to a Swedish buyer for a price lower than the value of the bronze it was made from. The atmosphere of that time with its slogans, meetings, marches, first of May and October parades will be recreated for those wanting to know about or wishing to be entertained by the whole ethos of the recent communist past of the country.

Similar ideas and projects in Poland and other former communist states are numerous, often ingenious and always heatedly debated. But while the debates continue in capital cities, towns and villages across Eastern Europe and the former Soviet Union, statues, busts, reliefs, murals and gigantic group sculptures are being destroyed. This is not a call to halt the executions or exiles of Socialist Realist works, not even a plea for closer scrutiny of their possible artistic merits. What is needed first of all is detailed documentation, then some discrete storage and display, not so much for the benefit of curious tourists, as for the continuity of material history and collective memory of the nations, for scholars researching the traumatic decades of Europe under communism and for art students and historians wishing to examine the alleged monstrosities, or perhaps simple mediocrity, of most Socialist Realist art.

ABOVE TO BELOW: Monument to the Army Engineers; Monument to the Soldiers of the First Army; OPPOSITE: To Brother-hood in Arms, 1945

NEW ART FROM SARAJEVO

CREATIVITY UNDER SIEGE
Kevin Weaver

Gaunt, haunting sculpted faces stare through glass portholes buried symbolically under a pile of Sarajevo's soil surrounded by trees made from broken glass. This is war art Sarajevo style. The installation by Mustafa Skopljak, a Muslim, is part of an exhibition called *Witnesses to Existence* of six established artists still working in Sarajevo. This is just one of four exhibitions currently being staged in Sarajevo which has even had the cheek to apply for the title of 'Cultural Capital of Europe' this year. This optimism and rich vein of creativity disproves the Latin adage that 'the muses are silent during times of war'.

Other exhibits included a poignant reminder of the dead and missing in the war which is a collage of faces from obituaries in the daily paper *Oslobedenja* or Nusret Pašić's 'Witnesses' which consists of a collection of dematerialised, infinitely elongated floating paper metaphysical figures. Unfortunately the gallery was hit by a shell forcing it to close temporarily. 'An arts embargo of a kind exists', says Rida Ettarahany, 28, a member of the video company Saga in Sarajevo. No artists can send works of art out of Sarajevo or attend exhibitions themselves abroad despite invitations from all over the world. The former minister for Health in France, who resigned in disgust at lack of real help for Bosnia, is now trying to open up a 'cultural corridor' between France and Bosnia to allow easy movement of works of art and artists. Louis Jammes, the French photographer, has already put up large photomontage posters of children embraced by angels, and is currently putting up another set of large photos of these pictures in place in Sarajevo. However his slightly pretentious statement 'The spirit of people in Sarajevo should be fed with culture', has angered many in Sarajevo and the car he was renting in Sarajevo was blown up by the boyfriend of his translator, with whom he was alleged to be having an affair!

The video company 'Saga' is the brainchild of Ademir Kenovic and it makes the daily five minute programmes on Channel 4 called 'A Street Under Seige' about the daily lives of those in Sarajevo, as well as many other documentaries such as the strikingly disturbing 'I burnt legs'. This was made by the promising young film maker, Srdjan Vuletic about the three months at the beginning of the war during which he worked at Kosevo hospital carrying the amputated limbs to the crematorium.

He also interviewed several amputees, one of whom was a young boy with one hand who tells of his distress at not being able to make a hard snowball!

Another strand of creativity currently thriving is the graphic design group TRIO, who have just used their own money to get 30,000 postcards and posters printed in Sarajevo along with 1,000 copies of a monthly magazine, *Cocktail*, that they have designed. Their infamous postcard 'Enjoy Sarajevo' using the Coca Cola logo, which is just one of their witty pop-art style postcards using icons and famous trademarks, has created quite a lot of interest internationally with articles appearing about them in *Newsweek*, *Paris Match* etc. They are now planning an exhibition of their posters in Sarajevo and maybe abroad to coincide with the tenth anniversary of the 1984 Winter Olympics which were held in Sarajevo, and at which Britons Torvill and Dean won their gold medal.

Other exhibitions taking place in Sarajevo are a collection of woodcut prints by 17 different artists at the 'Mak' Gallery, and an exhibition of children's paintings and drawings organised by UNICEF. Many of these pictures were done as part of art therapy classes organised by the International Red Cross as part of a new mental health project which includes the opening of nine centres to counsel mainly women and children traumatised by the war in Bosnia. In October 1993 there was an exhibition entitled 'War Architecture' showing photos of the many destroyed buildings in Sarajevo, and at the BiH Gallery there was an exhibition of photos by the *Vanity Fair* photographer Annie Leibovitz. In the Spring the Obala Gallery in Sarajevo will stage an exhibition of photos taken by the Magnum photographer Paul Lowe, and some of the World Press Photo Exhibition.

Although there is a great deal of art being produced for the four galleries still operating, one telling sign of the times is that one of the galleries has had to devote half its space to selling women's clothes to make ends meet. Unlike much art in the West, Sarajevo's art is ostensibly political. One of the more obvious examples is a picture of the European Community flag with a mortar protruding from the circle of stars. A cliché perhaps, but in this case art mirrors reality.

Installations at the exhibition Witness to Existence; *ABOVE & OPPOSITE work by Mustafa Skopljak BELOW: work by Nusret Pašić (photos by Kevin Weaver)*

THE STATUE OF LIBERTY'S SOUL

Tamás St Auby

On Mount St Gellért (750ft) in the centre of Budapest stands the Memorial of Liberation elevated on the orders of the Red Army in 1947. The monument (120ft), dominating the view of the whole town, has become an emblem of the new regime. During the revolution of 1956 the memorial was partly destroyed and after the suppression restored again.

Following the abolition of the one-party system in 1989, many Hungarians are demanding the removal of the monument for being a symbol of foreign repression, while many others are resisting its demolition for aesthetic or moral reasons.

The Bartók 32 Gallery, adopting the initiative of the situationist artist J Lorrensy, presented 'The Statue of Liberty's Soul Project' in November 1991 and with the moral and financial help of the Cultural Committee of Budapest, the gallery brought it into being on the 26 June 1992, coincid-

ing with the first anniversary of the Red Army's departure from Hungary. Professional mountain climbers wrapped the Statue of Liberty in plastic sheets giving it the strange and ghostly presence illustrated on the front cover of this magazine, its ephemeral appearance belied the accepted permanence of any monument. Accepting the controversies caused by the *Statue of Liberty's Soul*, its existence was limited to three days.

This project was submitted to Monumental Propaganda, *instigated by Komar and Melamid with* Artforum *and organised by ICI (Independent Curators Incorporated, New York). Komar and Melamid have long protested at the destruction of the commemorative monuments and memorials of the recently deposed Soviet regime, this project invited artists to 'collaborate with history' and make Soviet Socialist realism the subject of creative interrogations.*

LEFT: *Views of the* Statue of Liberty's Soul *in Budapest (original photos and mock up Tamás St Auby, reproductions László Lugosi Lugo); OPPOSITE:* The Statue of Liberty's Soul *in preparation (photo Tamás St Auby)*

ART AS A CONSCIOUS LIE
THE PAINTING OF ROBERT GEBETHNER
Piotr Choynowski

Born 1950, Robert Gebethner was part of the middle generation of Polish artists. He defines his art, his painting, as his attitude towards the world into which he happened to be born. His search for hints of something authentic is his way to survive, to be able to take a breath of fresh air in the otherwise stifling atmosphere of hypocrisy.

As he has said, pointing to his mentors, Bruno Schulz and Tadeusz Kantor,

It is not my aim to create anything new, I rather try to find the traces of something really real. Through painting it is possible to put in motion the forces of imagination which sometimes allow us to grasp the real, the true, at least on the personal level. Usually it happens by uncovering things that are unwanted, shameful or considered as trivial, but which in reality represent the world opposed to or rejected by conventions and as such more real.

Accordingly he researches the humble, the refused, the layers of dust amassed in the crevices of great systems, to unmask convention or reveal artifice masquerading as truth, to visualise the reality of convention. Gebethner works in series based on a leading motif, for example doodling: 'Doodling fascinates and inspires me by its lack of purpose, its disinterestedness as well as its fragility. Any attempt to arrest its content or to give it a more permanent form, inevitably leads to its disappearance or death in the throngs of convention. So what I am trying to do is only to register its unsophistication.'

Some earlier series based on old photographs of important personages of their time, explored the conventional poses and gestures of its subjects, trying to visualise the necessity or rather inevitability of convention, in a way its truth.

In this way art shows itself to be a conscious convention. In Gebethner's interpretation art thus becomes a conscious lie. Only in this way, following Duchamp, we can approach the truth of art. In Gebethner's case this caused him to be marginalised. After he finished at the Academy of Fine Arts in Cracow in 1975, where he was one of the most celebrated students, he returned to his home town, Warsaw, to start an art group called Bok Wyspy together with two other young artists. The group soon established itself as one of the most promising young artist associations of the late 70s.

Prior to Solaridarity and martial law, artistic life in Poland basked in full innocence, in the sun of stately patronage. The occasional political incursions by some rude or unsophisticated official were treated as annoying and irritating but nothing more. The Gierek era was relatively liberal and any declarations of political loyalty were not required nor was art coerced to follow the official dogma. This oasis within the totalitarian situation was shattered first by the emergence of the Solidarity movement and later by the imposition of martial law. The innocence was lost. With all pretensions gone, the artist suddenly found himself face to face with reality and this reality looked like a raw power and nothing else. Now it became necessary to declare oneself, to take sides, a frightening, but also an invigorating experience. In practice one was left with three possibilities: to respond positively to the governmental wooing, to go underground, or to do neither and retreat into oneself.

The first possibility tempted with continuing official patronage, the second with its moral and patriotic overtones, while the third, seemingly the least attractive, could show itself to be artistically the most rewarding. The two main options were not free of some degree of social opportunism, while the third gave the artist an occasion to rethink and reassess. It is thus not surprising, that many have chosen precisely this and among them Robert Gebethner.

This choice reflected his general attitude which was concentrated around the problem of truth, convention and truth conventionalised. The last refers to politics, where the conventionalised 'truths' are the main instrument of manipulation. So, for Gebethner the world of official as well as underground politics, did not seem very sympathetic, with the obvious propaganda of the one and the martyrological colouring of the other. To be sure it did not mean a total isolation. Though the official exhibiting was boycotted by the majority among the artistic community, there were exhibitions held in private flats and churches. Gebethner took part and even organised some of them.

With the collapse of communism, the artistic life of the country came to life again. The group Bok Wyspy was revived, becoming in the meantime something of a classic, especially in the eyes of the young generation.

However, the new situation with the emerging market economy posed new and not quite expected problems. Paradoxically under the old regime, art enjoyed not only an official support but was authentically cherished by the public at large, which sought in it a relief from a drab and monotonous existence. The social standing of an artist was incomparable with that of his equivalent in the West. In many ways he really held command over the soul of the nation. The shift from that exalted position to becoming a producer of commodities, with commercial success or its lack, totally depending on utterances of a critic or the goodwill of a well connected gallery, must have been dramatic. For Gebethner it may seem like a confirmation of his philosophy where one system of conventions is replaced by another. The political propaganda systems were exchanged for commercial ones. Gebethner's quest remains as valid as ever.

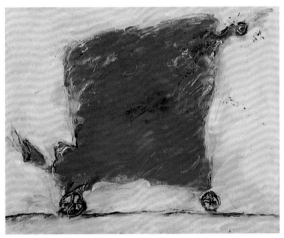

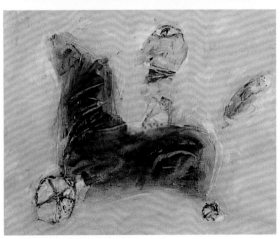

FROM ABOVE L TO R: A Vehicle 1, *1993, oil, 35x40cm;* A Vehicle 2, *1993, oil, 35x40cm;* In the Car, *1993, oil, 35x40cm;* The Ride, *1993, oil, 100x80cm;* The Small Car, *1993, oil, 35x40cm;* The Horseman, *1993, oil, 35x40cm*

JIŘÍ KOLÁŘ
DICTIONNAIRE DES MÉTHODES
Vivian Constantinopoulos

EVIDENCE POEMS ('SCHWITTERSIADS')
Before I understood Schwitters's collages, the pictorial poems of Jiri Voskovec made my head spin. Schwitters haunted me until I made several collages in his honor. I ran into him head-on when I came back from a trip to Hannover in 1966. A great deal of correspondence had piled up at home, and while sorting it out, I felt the word 'Merz' in my mouth. What was on the table was a testimony of my absence. I began to collect paper that bore witness to my day or week (Diary 1967). This included not only newspaper clippings, but also tram and bus tickets, receipts, letters, lists, notes – evidence of my day. Arranged and glued down, they formed an 'evidence poem'.

PROSTHETIC POEMS
If it is possible for man to survive with artificial limbs, the same possibility exists for life in general, and for modern art in particular. When I was working on the 'Killed' collages, I had long reflected on the end of things or on their flight. I had also encountered the enigma of predestination and the blueprint of birth. This is why, for example, I would replace the amputated parts of a 'crumplage' with an undestroyed reproduction, a collage, a 'chiasmage' or vice-versa.

(Extracts from *Jiří Kolář*, Milan: Giancarlo Politi Editore, 1986)

Descartes's *Discours de la méthode* shows that the method of systematic doubt can be employed to lead eventually to a truth that is beyond and immune to scepticism. Descartes's chain of reasoning leads to his most famous principle: 'Cogito, ergo sum'. Method is used as a way forward. In Jiří Kolář's collage work *Dictionnaire des méthodes*, the idea of a doctrine is likewise rejected in favour of methods. But instead, as his title states, Kolář is dealing with not one but many methods, and all of them are ways of suggesting new and potential aspects in art.

Kolář's work, spanning the greater part of this century, comprises text and pictures – from poems written throughout the 30s, 40s and 50s, to collages of pictures gathered from art-history books and magazines. Indeed, his name itself is a testimony to both his visual art and the art of language, for the name Kolář, pronounced in Czech, sounds equivalent to 'collage'. His decision to work in a pictorial medium should not be regarded as a rejection of language however, but rather as a negotiation with language (to the extent where one might 'feel' 'the word "Merz" in my mouth' as Kolář mentions in the piece above), one that would go through and beyond language to reach new meanss of communication in pictures. The collages, in which Kolář uses a variety of techniques which he names 'rapportages', 'crumplages', 'confrontages', 'rollages', etc, are suggestive rather than descriptive, carrying fragments of history and ideas that are incorporated into each collage's own world – and Kolář's own world – and then put forward to the viewer for a further use in his or her own experience.

In addition to being seen as a negotiation with language, his pictorial work also embraces poetry.

As Descartes's *Discourse* was a way of attaining truth in science, Kolář's *Dictionary* is an attempt to discover the poetry in the world around us. By acknowledging the fundamental meaning of 'poetry' – that of 'poiesis': making, creating – we find that what concerns Kolář is not merely presenting a list of quotations (whether visual or verbal) by utilising and amassing images we have already seen, but instead putting forward a series of collages, themselves each made up of a multitude of pictures, to show that an exploration of these pictures can then be used to create new questions in the viewer and new ways of seeing. The methods themselves are multiple and, as Gilbert Lascault writes, become the rules of a game: 'Instead of making the artistic work "sacred", or the outcome of some kind of incommunicable inspiration, the artist shows us how serious games of invention are organised; he specifies the rules that are laid down while at the same time giving himself the right to change the rules and the right to switch from one rule to another, even in the middle of the game.' (Gilbert Lascault, 'Sept notes en marge du livre et des oeuvres de Jiří Kolář'.)

Kolář's works – his dictionary of methods – are therefore formed of rules but not of compromises; his 'games' of collages can be modified and adjusted. There exists no hierarchy in the form of the dictionary; there are merely entries under each letter, which can then all be added to ad infinitum. Moreover, the changes are to be made by the spectators in their interpretations, for the collages, although Kolář's 'creation', are there to be shared, as indeed the copies of the various images from which he has constructed his work circulate amongst many, as inspiration to each spectator's own poetic language and vision.

Mikhail Bakhtin has written: 'The writer is a person who knows how to work language while remaining outside of it; he has the gift of indirect speech'. Furthermore, the writer 'does not experience [the event], but co-experiences it, since the event cannot be viewed as such unless, in some measure, we participate in it by evaluating it. This exotopy (which is not indifference) allows artistic creativity to give the event unity, form, and completion from outside' (from T Todorov's *Mikhail Bakhtin: The Dialogical Principle*, Univ of Minnesota Press, 1984, pp 68 and 100). In Kolář's case, indirect speech becomes a way of direct communication. He has the artistic ability to communicate his own pictorial language as a prompt for his audience to recognise what they can from his assemblages; not through necessarily asking questions himself, but producing questions in his own audience for them to ask. The viewers themselves can then add their own methods and findings to the *Dictionary* – a work in continuous process.

Exhibition: *Jiří Kolář – Dictionnaire des méthodes*, Fundació Joan Miró, Barcelona, Dec 93-Jan 1994.

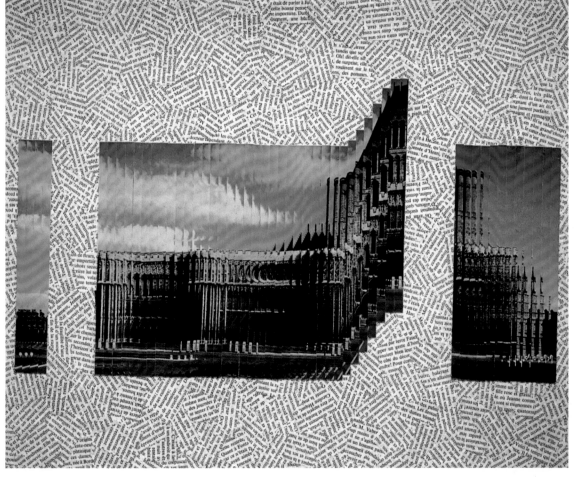

FROM ABOVE L TO R:
Décalligrammes: sans les vieillards, *1982;* Disformations, inaperceptions, collages détraqués: samedi 9 mars, 1991 (Murillo)*, 1991;* Collage hebdomadaire: collage commencé dans le train, *1982;* Amputations: la cathédrale endormie, *1982*

TOK BORN by AD Richards, Tok Publication, 40pp, HB £11.95 PB £5.95

Tok's major aim is to experiment with the visual representation of writing. This emphasis makes Tok different from standard literary and typographic journals. This is not just an aesthetic consideration but an attempt to find common principles that can relate typography to writing within an eclectic format. Dr Gaele Sobott-Mogwe claims that the ideas presented through Tok challenge the 'rigid divisions between prose and poetry: the staid expectations of form and presentation are blurred and out of this undefined space emerges the beauty of expression that is so often denied, unrecognised, ignored'. Clara Allen's poem *Equal Shares* is divided into two columns to enhance the meaning of the words. The feelings discussed in the dialogue comprising Will D Downing's *Firstborn* are described with equal effect by the typography and words to a mutually beneficial end.

ARTS TV – A History of Arts Television in Britain by John A Walker, The Arts Council of Great Britain, b&w ills, 243pp, PB £17.50

This is the first general, systematic history to identify the various types or genres of arts programmes – review programmes and series, drama documentaries, artists' profiles, etc – and then gives a chronological account of their evolution from 1936 to the 1990s. Important art series like *Civilisation*, *Ways of Seeing*, *Shock of the New*, *State of the Art* and *Relative Values* are described in detail. There are also chapters on art educational programmes and computer graphics. A recurrent issue is the representation of the fine arts – 'high', minority culture in a 'low' mass culture medium. Art TV brings art to a wider audience than just the art critics. Programmes such as the 50-minute Warhol documentary in 1973 excited public controversy and prompted legal proceedings over accusations of bad language, nudity and transvestitism. On the other hand, the title of Robert Hughes' major series *The Shock of the New* was considered to be misleading since that which it contained was neither shocking or new. The *Showcases for Artists*

work were perhaps the most successful, since they did not attempt subjective comment but left the viewers to decide.

CHARLES KEEPING An Illustrator's Life by Douglas Martin, Julia MacRae Books, colour ills, 255pp, HB £40

This book celebrates the life and work of Charles Keeping, one of the most influential modern book illustrators, who died in 1988. Keeping was a Londoner through and through, and his childhood in Lambeth provided him with an endlessly rich source to draw on throughout his working life. But his vision was universal, individual and often disturbing – the strength and honesty of everything he undertook changed the face of British children's book illustration. His powerful sense of observation is revealed in studies of facial expression and body language in *The Latchkey Children*, 1963. His facility with simple lines can be seen in his pictures for *Little Dorrit* where without using shading or colour he achieves convincing spatial relationships that create a powerful pattern. His fascination for the macabre is expressed through concentrated mood interpreted through line to a violent and extraordinary effect.

THAT'S THE WAY I SEE IT by David Hockney, Thames and Hudson, colour ills, 248pp, HB £24.95

'I have always believed that art should be a deep pleasure . . . There is always, everywhere, an enormous amount of suffering, but I believe that my duty as an artist is to overcome and alleviate the sterility of despair . . . New ways of seeing mean new ways of feeling . . . I do believe that painting can change the world'. Over the past 20 years, David Hockney has devoted himself to forging a new way of seeing through an intense and impassioned exploration of a variety of forms and mediums: painting, drawing, stage design, photography and printmaking. This colourful book surrounds each image with detailed accounts of personal experience and artistic endeavour making it one of the most revealing autobiographies of a modern artist. For example, on a page with images of Tristan and Isolde painted while he was involved with

the staging of that opera in Los Angeles 1987, Hockney reveals that he painted these images for himself to put the characters into models for his studio and bring them alive for him while he designed the set.

TEKSTURA Russian Essays on Visual Culture edited and translated by Alla Efimova and Lev Manovich, University of Chicago Press, b/w ills, 231pp, HB £ 27.95 PB £10.25

Taking its title from a Russian word that can refer to the 'texture' of life, painting, or writing, this collection of essays represents an important cross section of art history and cultural theory by Russian language writers. They erase the boundaries between high and low, official and dissident, avant-garde and socialist realism. In his foreword, Stephen Bann describes the context for the West's fascination with the myth of the Russian avant-garde. Alla Efimova and Lev Manovich relate the insights of the Russian writers to the quest for interpretive approaches to visual culture, images and vision. Everything visual is deemed worthy of analysis, whether painting or propaganda banners, architecture or candy wrappers, mass celebrations or urban refuse. Chapters discuss Stalinism as an aesthetic phenomenon; the conceptual installation of Ilya Kabakov; architectural discussions are debated in chapters on paper architecture and on the relations between the public and the artist in Russia at the turn of the 20th Century.

WHAT IS ART? Experience art in the world around you by Rosemary Davidson, Oxford University Press, b/w and colour ills, 128pp, HB £12.99

This ambitious publication sets out to teach art appreciation in an informal and interesting way and to encourage children to develop a confident approach to forming their own opinions about art. It is organised thematically into a systematic analysis of the lives and works of painters, sculptors and other craftspeople and examines their work and the techniques they employ. Davidson's engaging style and imaginative approach can be seen through her lateral analysis. In the chapter 'Magic and Making

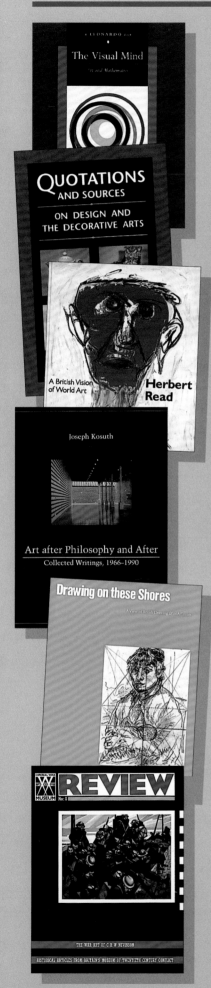

Things Happen' she examines the subject through different cultures: the magic scarabs of the Ancient Egyptians, the North African metal hand worn as protection from the evil eye and the shaman rattle used on the Northwest Coast of America.

THE VISUAL MIND Art and Mathematics edited by Michele Emmer, MIT Press (A Leonardo Book) b/w and colour ills, 274pp, HB £35.95

Scientific visualisation, higher-dimensional geometries, three-dimensional computer modelling, computer animation and virtual environments are just a few of the areas in which artists and mathematicians are exchanging ideas and working together. This book is written by mathematicians concerned with the visual fruits of their computations and by visual artists concerned with the mathematical origins and inspirations of their works. The sections cover geometry and visualisation; computer graphics, geometry and art: symmetry and perspective, mathematics and art. The book introduces the increasingly important area of computer graphics providing an insight into the impact such methods of generation will have in the future. Throughout the book three dimensional shapes appear with slightly different features in an attempt to analyse the way we imagine forms in our mind's eye. Chromaticity diagrams present data and formulae to rationalise our perception of colour. Patterns of symmetries and uneven groupings provide a matrix on which to form such perceptions.

QUOTATIONS AND SOURCES On Design and the Decorative Arts compiled by Paul Greenhalgh, Manchester University Press, 240pp, HB £35 PB £9.95

This book brings together key writings from leading designers, artists and critics from the period 1760 to the present day, ranging from short quotes to longer extracts. These are organised chronologically within thematic sections which directly relate to contemporary areas of concern within the visual arts: ornament, political and social reform, technology, craft, race and national identity, Modernism, and aesthetics. It contains extracts from the writings and

speeches of personalities such as Josiah Wedgwood, William Morris, Frank Lloyd Wright, Le Corbusier, Eileen Gray, Alvar Aalto, Judy Chicago, Terence Conran, Ron Arad, Charles Jencks and HRH the Prince of Wales.

HERBERT READ A British Vision of World Art edited by Benedict Read and David Thistlewood, Lund Humphries in association with Leeds City Art Galleries and the Henry Moore Foundation, colour ills, 182pp, PB £18

In a passage entitled 'A Nest of Gentle Artists' Herbert Read likens himself to a circus rider with his feet planted astride two horses, referring to his equal allegiance to different groupings among the 1930s artistic avant-garde of London. Like his friend TS Eliot, Read quickly made a reputation as a literary critic, but, lacking private means, he needed a career. Eliot chose banking, Read the Civil Service though he soon gravitated to museum curatorship. His views were profoundly influenced by his personal friendships and the intellectual circles in which he moved. Meeting Moore and Hepworth and Nicholson changed his life. They stimulated his own creativity, and fuelled his 'naturally dialectic way of thinking'.

ART AFTER PHILOSOPHY AND AFTER Collected Writings of Joseph Kosuth 1966-1990 edited by Gabriele Guercio, MIT Press, b/w ills, 289pp, PB £14.95 (new ed)

Joseph Kosuth's writings, like his installations, assert that art begins where mere physicality ends. The articles, statements and interviews collected here produced over a period of 24 years range from discussions on the philosophy of language to anthropology, Marxism and linguistics. He aims to discover the common principles that inform representation while negotiating the endlessly complex debates about art of the last two decades. Rooted in Freud, Wittgenstein and French theory, Kosuth's work investigates the linguistic nature of art propositions and the role of social, institutional, psychological and ethnological context. Gabriele Guercio suggests that as a whole his writings present a new definition of an expanded role and responsibility for the artist.

In his foreword, Jean-François Lyotard asks, 'A man takes his finger, a stick, or a paintbrush, plunges it into an oxide paste or an ink, and draws some strokes on a support. Is he writing or painting?'

DRAWING ON THESE SHORES A View of British Drawing and its Affinities by Glenn Sujo, Harris Museum and Art Gallery, b/w ills, 72pp, PB £6.95

Ford Madox Brown's self-portrait reveals the code of propriety and moral reticence of the Victorian age. Its truth to reality is typical of Pre-Raphaelite philosophy, to which he subscribed. Drawings are often in preparation for paintings; however with the increasing abstraction of art, the importance of harnessing spontaneity increasingly caused them to be considered as the end product. Mark Tobey's *Composition*, 1958, is an example of this tendency and the rhythmical pattern of incisions has been interpreted as having a mystical quality. Stanley Spencer and Colin Gill represent one of the strongest veins of British art, and their drawings show the build up of energy of their final work. Henry Moore's sketches achieve a sturdy quality evident in his sculptural work.

REVIEW NO 8 The War Art of CRW Nevinson principally by the staff of The Imperial War Museum, colour ills, 111pp, PB £9.90

This series of journals charts the different effects war had and has on our cultural lives. In his essay, 'The Empty Battlefield', Paul Gough examines Paul Nash's *Menin Road*. He examines empirical, photographic and documentary records of the topography of the Western Front at that time in order to construct a comparative analysis of the subject. He applies this approach to a variety of famous war artists including Edward Handley Read and Ian Strang. Gough quotes John Masefield's powerful description of the battlefield 'a dressing on a kind of putrid box that was cankering the whole earth'. In 'The War Art of CRW Nevinson', Charles Doherty quotes a letter from Nevinson to Major Lee, 'I am writing to ask you if you would be good enough to let me have an idea of your ideal type of manly beauty as I have just heard that you have censored one of my best

pictures as "too ugly".'

COMPULSIVE BEAUTY by Hal Foster, MIT Press, b/w ills, 313pp, PB £22.50

Foster works from the premise that surrealism 'has long been seen', as its founder André Breton wanted it to be seen, as a movement of love and liberation. Foster attempts to restage the difficult encounter of surrealism with Freudian psychoanalysis to redefine the crucial categories of surrealism – the marvellous, convulsive beauty, objective chance – in terms of the Freudian uncanny. He develops the idea that the surrealist image is derived from the analysis of primal fantasy. He examines the social dimension of surrealism formed through its connection with mechanisation and commodification. He consults the surrealist use of outmoded images as an attempt to work through the historical repression effected by these same processes. Foster claims that this is a deconstructive reading of surrealism which addresses the neglected area of its involvement with desire and trauma, capitalist shock and technological development. This claim to novelty is unconvincing, though the numerous anecdotes which allow for subjective interpretation are very thought provoking.

CHRISTIAN BOLTANSKI by Lynn Gumpert, Flammarion, colour ills, 182pp, PB £20

Christian Boltanski has created a substantial body of work out of insubstantial objects that represent the preoccupations that haunt him: the way photographs can lie, nostalgia for a childhood that must disappear, parodies on the idea of collecting the presence of death, memory and forgetting. Boltanski's disconcerting oeuvre invokes funerary sculptures and public memorials. They are not constructed out of stone but from small tin-framed photographs arranged in geometrical, often symmetrical configurations. He undermines the traditional idea of a monument by the tangled web of black wires leading to small bulbs which detract from the geometry. His interpretation of the *Bougies* uses miniature metal figures and candles on a shelf perpendicular to the wall to dramatic effect mak-

ing it seem that the elongated the shadows cast, dance.

ART WITHOUT REJECTION by Sheila Reid, Rush Editions, b/w ills, 242pp, PB $22.95

She claims that vast numbers of people have begun to turn to art for something extra in their life. 'I met a man the other day who said he was an artist. He was sure his costume defined the role he was playing, black fedora hat, mauve shirt, pink flowery tie, cranberry jacket and a bright red cashmere scarf. I think he was really an arms dealer or something.' Since art has become a glamourous industry, certain dealers have taken advantage of the situation turning their personal taste into an indispensable product, not necessarily for its artistic depth or spiritual value but for their own profits and pride. With this book Reid aims to provide a formula to empower genuine artists and prevent them from having to live under the negative atmosphere of constant rejection. Artists report that Sheila Reid's method of organising exhibitions without giving anyone the right to reject their artwork is nothing short of a miracle. The idea of artists earning and investing in areas outside of art, both to have an independent income and to stimulate their creative abilities and their self-respect has surprised everyone. Since she proposes that artists pay great attention to whom they allow to handle or own their artwork, a debate has begun over who should have power over art, the merchants or the artists? Her proposals for empowering the artists are based on 20 years of experience of protecting her artworks from abuse and ensuring that they are placed in museums where they are appreciated by the largest public.

ANDY WARHOL Portraits by Henry Geldzahler and Robert Rosenblum, Thames and Hudson, colour ills, 168pp, HB £28

The portraits of Andy Warhol, the undisputed champion of American Pop Art, are the fruits of one of his most significant creative periods. The 'icon' of the series, Marilyn Monroe, appeared as early as 1962. From then until the last year of his life, Warhol created a virtual museum of personalities,

both living and deceased, from the worlds of film, show business, art, literature and politics. Characteristic of Warhol's unique style of portraiture is the use of silkscreens made from polaroid photographs – some of which were taken by the artist during encounters with his subjects at the notorious Factory. Warhol then primed his canvases with a rich repertoire of colours, both bold and expressionistic. Among the best-known sitters shown here are Truman Capote, David Hockney, John Lennon, Judy Garland, Rudolph Nureyev, Prince Charles and Princess Diana.

ART OF THE ELECTRONIC AGE by Frank Popper, Thames and Hudson, colour ills, 192pp, HB £24.95

Art has been the subject of more explosive experimentation in the last 20 years than in almost any other period. Not only have most preconceptions about art and the artist been questioned and sometimes overturned; whole new media and areas of artistic activity have been pioneered, especially since the advent of such technology as the personal computer, Xerox, video and lasers. Frank Popper divides the subject into five categories: laser and holographic art; video art; computer art; communication art; and installation, demonstration and performance art. He analyses these movements in terms of their objectives and the artists who take part in them. The illustrations are an essential aspect of this analysis, for they often show what cannot be described by words alone. What is most fascinating about these works is that, although their creators are experimenting with ways and means undreamt of even 50 years ago, their objective is the same as that of artists since antiquity – to create a shared aesthetic.

ART & BUSINESS by Marjory Jacobson, Thames and Hudson, colour ills, 224pp, HB £32

In the uncertain economic climate of the 1990s, why should corporations turn their workplaces into centres of cultural excellence? Great or small, the leaders in this field share one fundamental characteristic: they all know the value of taking risks and setting standards. Their art programmes are

highly sophisticated management tools geared to enlightened self-interest. Some businesses have established their own museums, and many more companies have not only embellished their interiors with high-quality collections but have also sponsored artists' involvement in the production of business reports, advertising campaigns and training strategies. Over 40 case studies are organised into eight major themes to identify the corporate benefits of patronage.

AFRICAN ART IN TRANSIT by Christopher B Steiner, Cambridge University Press, b/w ills, 220pp, HB £35 PB £16.95
This book examines how art objects achieve meaning and value as they travel across cultural and international boundaries. It addresses anthropology, art history, sociology and economics. Steiner explains that African art dealers are aware of the discovery element in Western taste and will feign naivety to allow the buyer to believe that the dealer is not aware of the significance and value of the artifact. The concept of authenticity is approached from many angles, one of which is explained through an anecdote involving a tourist who wanted to swap his Seiko watch for a 'Dan face mask' and was anxious to establish that it was 'real'. While he examined the mask for signs of use and age the dealer examined his watch for scratches and 'hall marks'.

FROM MANET TO MANHATTAN The Rise of the Modern Art Market by Peter Watson, Vintage, b/w ills, 558pp, PB £9.99
The introduction has the dramatic immediacy of a blockbuster novel as Peter Watson takes us behind the scenes at the Christie's auction. Concentrating on paintings as well as books and Oriental art, this is a probing analysis of the art market during the past century. Watson portrays the rise of the auction houses, the recent and spectacular involvement of the Japanese, and also the development of the 'dealers, flamboyant salesmen, fastidious scholars and some downright crooks'. This book also includes some interesting statistics: the most expensive painting sold between 1913-14 was Raphael's *Panshanger Madonna*;

between 1928-29, Raphael's *Large Panshager Madonna*; between 1959-1960, Rubens' *Adoration of the Kings* and between 1987-1990, Van Gogh's *Portrait of Dr Gachet*, sold for a world record price of $82.5 million.

FIN DE SIECLE Art and Society in an Age of Uncertainty by Shearer West, Bloomsbury, colour ills, 153pp, HB £20
The forthcoming decade of uncertainty and experiment is not only characteristic of our time, but has dominated the century's end throughout modern Western history. Conflicting feelings of hope and anxiety, expression and repression, continuity and change have dominated fin de siècle societies and have emerged as the focus of art and literature. From the basis of the art of the late 19th century, Shearer West examines this cultural phenomenon throughout the history of the Western World. By unlocking the hidden meanings located in images of women, men, sexuality, despair and death, we can not only recover the obsessions of a past age, but reach a greater understanding of our own.

PARAGONS OF VIRTUE Women and Domesticity in Seventeenth-Century Dutch Art by Wayne E Franits, Cambridge University Press, colour ills, 272pp, HB £40
This is the first systematic analysis of paintings of domestic themes, which were among the most popular and endearing images produced by Dutch artists during the Golden Age. Focusing on their broader function and significance within Dutch culture, this study has made extensive use of 16th- and 17th-century family treatises that are important sources for understanding these paintings. These hortatory texts are significant because they reflect contemporary attitudes towards women as they are paradigmatically presented as maidens, as housewives skilled in the administration of household affairs, as attentive mothers and as pious widows. This book sheds further light on the position of women in 17th-century Dutch society and on the critical role that art played in early modern Europe in espousing and maintaining the patriarchal status quo.

COLOUR AND CULTURE Practice and Meaning from Antiquity to Abstraction by John Gage, Thames and Hudson, colour ills, 333pp, HB £38
From the ancient Greeks to the late 20th century, John Gage considers the vast range of colour and its meaning in different cultures. He describes the first theories of colour, articulated by philosophers from Democritus to Aristotle, and subsequent attempts by the Romans and their Renaissance disciples to organise it systematically or endow it with symbolic power. Gage analyses its religious significance as an incarnation of the Divine Light in the mosaics and stained glass of Byzantine and medieval Christianity and its use in heraldry, as part of a language of coded signs. He shows how the great artists of the Renaissance approached colour with the help of their contemporaries, the alchemists who invested it with all kinds of magical and spiritual properties. He explores the experimental analysis of the spectrum undertaken by Newton and continued in the 19th century by artists such as Seurat. Gage traces the influence of Goethe's colour theory and developments as diverse as Matisse's exploration of complementary shades and the manufacture of paints.

BORDERLANDS Contemporary Photography from the Baltic States, Street Level Photography Gallery, b/w ills, 100pp, PB £9.95
The Lighthouse Media Centre in Wolverhampton is the final venue for a touring exhibition of photography from around the Baltic States. Throughout the 50 years of Soviet rule, which came to an end in 1991, these countries clung doggedly to their individual identities. They now find themselves exposed to Western images and ideologies. It is this crossroads that 'Borderlands' addresses. No longer bound by state restrictions, photographers became free to use the medium in a fine-art, even conceptual, way. Lithuanian Vytautis Stanionis, for example, prints up negatives taken by his father for Soviet passports – two by two, to save film. Other works explore more personal, even spiritual, visions as well as the political events of recent years.

A selection of volumes to be published by Academy Editions in the summer of 1994

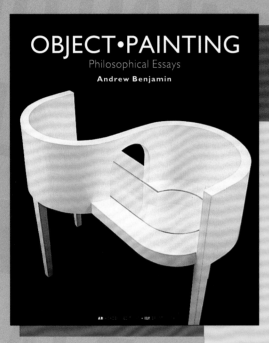

OBJECT•PAINTING
Philosophical Essays
Andrew Benjamin

*A*ndrew Benjamin, who has been described as one of the most original philosophers writing today, offers in this book a sustained and unique interpretation of painting and the question of the art object. Both topics raise questions central to the understanding of art in the 20th century: the relationship of painting to time; the continuing influence of Duchamp on the art object, the increasing use of installation as an art form and the instability of the categories of painting and sculpture that emerges from the project of minimalism. The book discusses the work of a diverse selection of artists from different generations including Anselm Kiefer, Jackson Pollock, Gerhard Richter, Robert Ryman, Christian Boltanski, Langlands and Bell.

PB 1 85490 361 6
297 x 217mm, 144 pages
50 illustrations, mainly in colour
Publication date: July 1994

'*T*his book is an argument in pictures for the centrality of architecture and art to what is human and to what might be constructed subsequent to what it has been to be human'.

Continuing the collaboration for over 30 years between Arakawa and Madeline Gins, this book is a unique and predominantly visual exploration into architecture which carries philosophical argument into the realm of construction. It asks what is the nature of perception in images of architectural constructions, how does the human being relate to the surrounding space? This is the first systematic study of the role that body and bodily movement play in the forming of the world; the reader is taken on a visual journey through a series of computer-generated images of great beauty and intricacy. The book presents readers with ways of reworking the man-made world that is architecture: floors become terrains and areas of undefined space are replaced by positional markers, horizons are constructed in duplicate or triplicate either to mirror or contradict one another. The book suggests a revolutionary re-invention of the planet and by extension the universe arguing that architecture is central to human life.

PB 1 85490 279 2
305 x 252mm, 144 pages
Full colour
Publication date: July 1994
An Art & Design Monograph

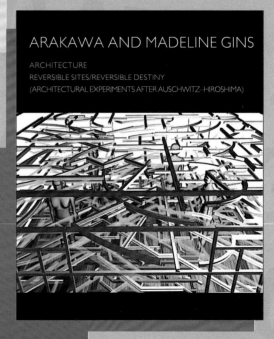

ARAKAWA AND MADELINE GINS

ARCHITECTURE
REVERSIBLE SITES/REVERSIBLE DESTINY
(ARCHITECTURAL EXPERIMENTS AFTER AUSCHWITZ–HIROSHIMA)

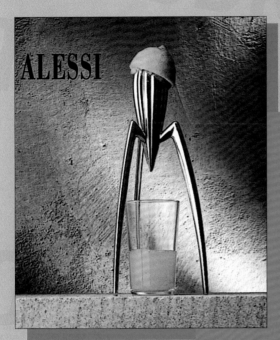

During the 1980s the Alessi company emerged at the forefront of design activity. Founded in 1921 to produce crafted products in metal for eating and drinking, Alberto Alessi launched the company into the design decade through his unique collaboration with designers and architects such as Sottsass, Sapper, Castiglioni and Mendini and the creation of two main trade marks: 'Alessi', geared towards mass production and 'Officina Alessi' towards more experimental limited editions. Alberto Alessi discusses the company's design ethos, viewing it as a research laboratory in the Applied Arts, Michael Graves and Alessandro Mendini provide their own personal views, as do many of the designers who have worked with Alessi. Daniel Weil writes from an academic point of view, and Nonie Niesewand from that of a design editor. All the famous products are illustrated and much less well known and unpublished material is also included. Following the rebuttal of the design decade, this book shows how Alessi flourishes and develops into the 1990s.

PB 1 85490 334 9
305 x 252mm, 144 pages
Over 200 illustrations, mainly in colour
Publication date: June 1994
An Art & Design Monograph

Audio Arts, the invention of two artists William Furlong and Barry Barker, began in 1973 as the first and only art magazine to be regularly published on audio cassette. It is now a unique and invaluable source of reference about contemporary art of the last 20 years including collaborations with leading international artists, interviews, discussion, art-works, documentation, reportage and archive recordings. *Definitions of Practice* draws together the extensive activities of Audio Arts demonstrating the great originality and complexity of this project which uses sound and the authenticity of the spoken word as its primary medium. More than simply being a mode of documentation that has the reality of a given time, with the impress of the participants' voices, the magazine was perceived as the carrier of real art-works in sound form. The artists, critics and authors featured here include Wyndham Lewis, James Joyce, WB Yeats, Marcel Duchamp, John Cage, Philip Glass, Yoko Ono, Jeff Koons, with major interviews and texts by Joseph Beuys, Richard Hamilton, Roy Lictenstein, Gerhard Richter, Richard Long, Ilya Kabakov and Anish Kapoor.

This is required reading for anyone with an interest in the last 20 years of art.

PB 1 85490 3632
305 x 252mm, 264 pages
Over 300 illustrations, mainly in colour
Publication date: July 1994

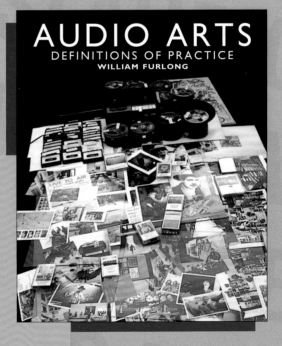

Further information can be obtained from Academy Group Ltd 071 402 2141

NEW HAPPENINGS

Art & Architecture in Russia and the Baltic States

NEW HAPPENINGS
Art & Architecture in Russia
and the Baltic States

*C*apturing an important moment in Russia's history, this book presents a view of recent developments in art and architecture in the context of the critical debates of postmodernism and national cultures. The return to popular national sources in the 1960s-80s was a means for Soviet artists, in a multi-ethnic state, to avoid submersion in the official ideology of 'Socialist Realism'. Thus the theme of Postmodernism not only enabled Soviet artists of this period to escape from the confines of official art, it also gave them a feeling of belonging to an international movement in the arts. The transition from totalitarianism to pluralism is evident in the diversity of work featured by both artists and architects from different regions of the former USSR. The influence of Eastern and Western cultures is apparent as is the divergence of generations. Essays by leading Russian and Western art and literary critics including Charles Jencks, Lisa Appignanesi, Elinor Shaffer, Alexander Rappaport, Alexei Tolstoy, Nadezhda Yurasovskaya, give a critical, historical and personal context to an exciting survey of work produced in Russia since the fall of communism – Art which reflects both the optimism and the apprehension of Russia as it approaches a momentous *fin de siècle*.

PB 1 85490 375 6
297 x 217mm, 144 pages
50 illustrations, mainly in colour
Publication date: July 1994

NEW ART FROM EASTERN EUROPE

NSK, Passport, *design: New Collectivism,* 1993

Art & Design

NEW ART FROM EASTERN EUROPE
IDENTITY AND CONFLICT

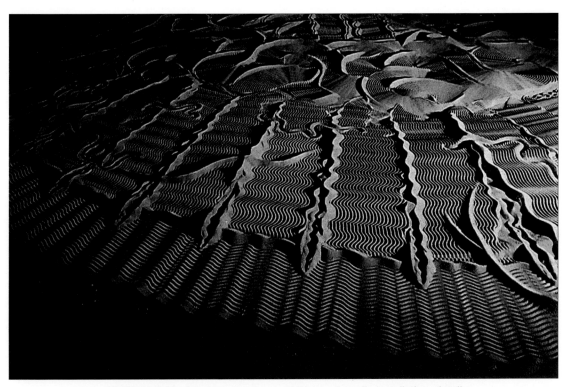

ABOVE: VSSD, Sand in your Eyes, *1991 mixed media installation, detail;*
OPPOSITE: Ilya Kabakov, 'The Man Who Flew into Space From His Apartment', from Ten Characters,
1981-88, detail, photo D James Dee, courtesy Ronald Feldman Fine Arts, New York

A.E. ACADEMY EDITIONS • LONDON

Acknowledgements

We would like firstly to thank Paul Crowther for guest-editing this special Eastern European issue of *Art & Design* and also Mojca Oblak for her considerable input, as well as all the other contributors for so generously giving their time and their energy to this project.

Introduction *pp6-7* p6 courtesy of the artist; **Neue Slowenische Kunst and New Slovenian Art** *pp8-17* images provided by author; **The Media and the War** *pp18-25* images courtesy of the artists; **Czech Art Today** *pp 26-35* p28 image courtesy Martin Polák; p29, p33 Zelda Cheatle Gallery; p31 Collection National Gallery of Canada, shown at 'Elective Affinities: The Language of the Body', 8 September – 7 November 1993, Tate Gallery, Liverpool; p35 both images from 'Europe Without Walls', Manchester City Art Galleries 13 November 93 – 16 January 94; **Milan Knížák** *pp36-43* images courtesy the artist; **A Communal Connection** *pp44-53* p46, p53, Illustration as a Way to Survive, Centre for Contemporary Arts, Glasgow, July – September 1993; p44, pp47-52 Ronald Feldman Fine Arts, New York; **Hungarian Conceptualism** *pp54-59* first published in *Joseph Kosuth: Zeno at the Edge of the Known World*, Palace of Exhibitions, Hungary, 1993, cat Hungarian Pavilion, Venice Biennale, with thanks to Dr Katalin Keserü; **Contemporary Polish Art** *pp60-71* all images courtesy the artists, pp62-63 Zacheta Gallery, Warsaw; **Mirosław Bałka** *pp72-75* We would like to thank Anda Rottenburg, curator of the Polish Pavilion at the Venice Biennale for her help in obtaining images; **The Enlightenment in Laibach** pp80-87 translated by Mojca Oblak, first published in the Croatian journal *Quorum*, 1987.

Notes on Contributors
Paul Crowther is a lecturer in art history at the University of St Andrews, he is the author of *Critical Aesthetics and Postmodernism,* 1993 and *Art and Embodiment: From Aesthetics to Self-Consciousness,* 1993, both published by Clarendon Press; **Mojca Oblak** is a Slovenian painter and theorist currently based in Scotland; **Marina Gržinić** is a Croatian video-artist and theorist, working in Ljubljana, Slovenia; **Ian McKay** teaches art history at Kingston University and has published numerous articles on East European art and other themes; **Johan Pijnappel** is a Dutch art historian and critic based in Amsterdam, he has guest-edited two previous issues of *Art & Design* magazine, *Fluxus* and *World Wide Video;* **Peter Suchin** is a painter and writer, he has published work in *Art Monthly, Variant* and other journals and is a member of the *Here and Now* magazine collective; **Éva Körner** is a Hungarian art historian based in Budapest; **Paulina Kolczynska** is a freelance writer and exhibitions organiser based in London and Warsaw; **William Furlong**, artist, publisher and lecturer is the founder of *Audio Arts* magazine which has been running since 1973; **Slavoj Žižek** is a researcher at the Institute of Sociology in the University of Ljubljana, Slovenia, he is the author of *The Sublime Object of Ideology* 1988, Verso, and *Looking Awry: An Introduction to Jacques Lacan through Popular Culture*, 1991, MIT Press.

Front Cover: Tamás St Auby, The Statue of Liberty's Soul Project, *1992, Budapest (photograph by László Lugosi Lugo); Inside Front and Back Covers: Milan Knížák,* New Paradise, *1990-91*

HOUSE EDITOR: Nicola Hodges EDITORIAL: Lucy Coventry
SENIOR DESIGNER: Andrea Bettella DESIGNER: Meret Gabra-Liddell

First published in Great Britain in 1994 by *Art & Design* an imprint of the
ACADEMY GROUP LTD, 42 LEINSTER GARDENS, LONDON W2 3AN
MEMBER OF THE VCH PUBLISHING GROUP

ISBN: 1 85490 218 0

Copyright © 1994 the Academy Group Ltd *All rights reserved*

The entire contents of this publication are copyright and cannot be reproduced
in any manner whatsoever without written permission from the publishers

The Publishers and Editor do not hold themselves responsible for the opinions expressed by the
writers of articles or letters in this magazine
Copyright of articles and illustrations may belong to individual writers or artists
Art & Design Profile 35 is published as part of *Art & Design* Vol 9 3/4 1994
Art & Design Magazine is published six times a year and is available by subscription

Printed and bound in Italy

Contents

Milan Knížák, Creature from New Paradise, *1992*

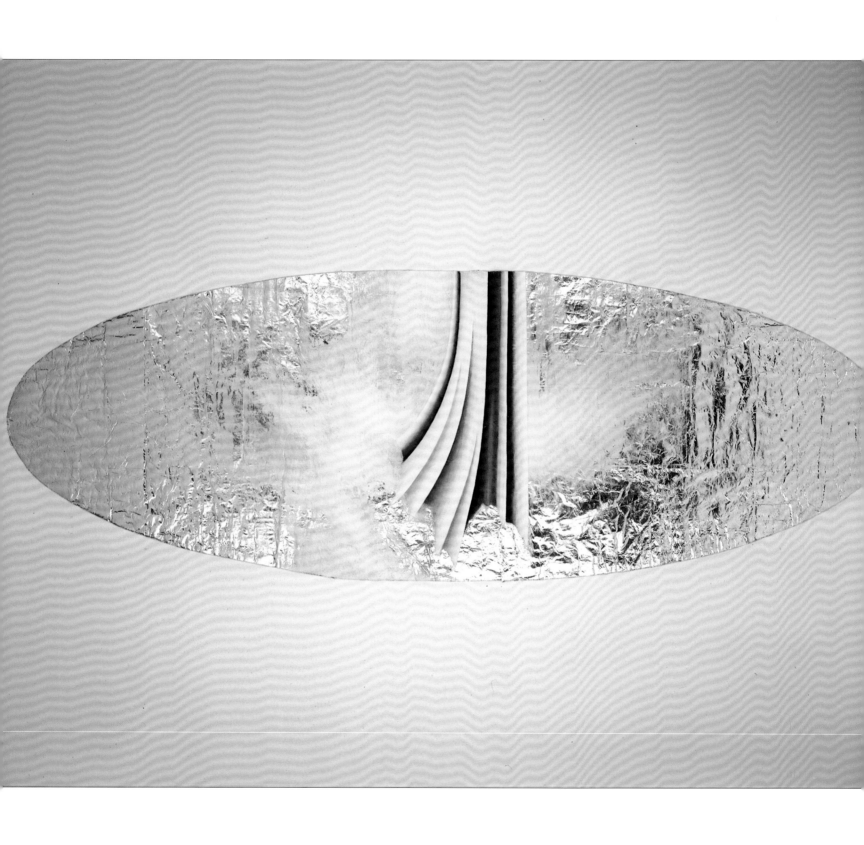

INTRODUCTION
PAUL CROWTHER

The purpose of the current issue of *Art & Design* is to introduce readers to art produced in Eastern Europe during and since the momentous events of the last decade. An encyclopedic treatment of this art is, of course, not possible in a single issue. We are content, therefore, to offer a cross-section of nations, individuals, and problems (both specific and much more general) which relate to the theme of conflict and identity.

A particular point of interest in the present issue is the special emphasis which it gives to works and ideas from two of the nations which have emerged (so bloodily) from the former Yugoslavia. This is timely – not only because the conflict there is (to say the least) on-going to a fatal degree, but also because that region has given rise to some of the strongest art yet produced in the postmodern era. In this respect, it is noteworthy that the first two contributions to this issue – Mojca Oblak and Marina Gržinić (from Slovenia and Croatia respectively) are at the forefront of a young generation of artists from the former Yugoslavia, who combine a commitment to practice, with a deep understanding of the more theoretical issues which it raises. Oblak's paper offers a useful general introduction to the question of conflict and identity, as well as addressing the specifically Slovenian context. Likewise, Gržinić, raises general issues about the relation between art, media, and warfare, as well as relating it specifically to events in Slovenia, Croatia and Bosnia.

This special emphasis in our Eastern European issue is finally expressed by a translation of Slavoj Žižek's paper relating Lacan to both the controversial Slovenian band Laibach and some more general themes. In the past few years Žižek has established himself as a leading Eastern European intellectual, and his work, of course, is now a major influence in the international scene. In my response to his paper, I shall develop some of his general themes as well as relating them back to specific aspects of East European art.

It goes without saying that the complex interplay between particular and general issues which inform the themes of conflict and identity, are also fully explored in the other articles in the present volume. Not least of these issues are the nature of the East's interaction with Western influences, and perhaps most acutely ambiguous of all, its new relation to the international art market. There is clearly a vast amount of market 'potential' in the former Eastern 'bloc', but whether or not the development of this will be of positive or negative value is a moot point. Ian McKay's article on Czech and Slovak art presents a very polemical treatment of this issue. The interview with Milan Knížák puts the matter in a somewhat different light. It is, of course, for the reader to decide his or her own position on this. Finally it is to be hoped that the art represented in this issue of *Art & Design* comes from creative sources which are practically and theoretically acute enough to retain their own distinctive voices. In this respect, the visual and theoretical evidence looks promising.

Mojca Oblak, Untitled, *1993, acrylic on foil, 170x140cm*

NEUE SLOWENISCHE KUNST

AND NEW SLOVENIAN ART
Mojca Oblak

In this paper, I am concentrating my attention on the Slovene artistic group NSK (Neue Slowenische Kunst), which in the last decade has been one of the strongest forces in Eastern European art generally. I will relate them to similar, but often radically different, artistic strategies in a broader Eastern European context. NSK's theories open a series of paradoxes, which are – through insistent references to totalitarianism – not just related to the question of the East/West relation, but seem to be intrinsic to basic social determinations of art in general.

On the other hand, that difference between East and West which defines cultural identity (and constitutes a collective undercurrent in a country like Slovenia) in a sense cannot be generalised at all. Cultural identity is a complex question which resists simplification in terms of an opposition to the other per se. This ideology of difference – expressed in the East/West conflict – seems to be a key question in general discussions on art in Eastern Europe, but because most Slovenian art is related to broader historical, social and artistic dimensions, its interpretation exceeds the given national, political or cultural frame. There are some common characteristics, of course, but they cannot be equalised in terms of cultural identity. Indeed, the more specific and often theoretically highly articulated motives behind this art are so diverse that I am unable to do full justice to them in a study of this length.

It seems that discussion concerning Eastern European art demands consideration of the recently developed 'democratic' tendencies in the area. No matter how often they are analysed, problems such as the disappearance of socialism from Eastern Bloc countries, the decay of the eschatology of communism, the disintegration of Yugoslavia, the fall of the Berlin wall etc, cannot be avoided, so that the situation of post totalitarianism, with its disillusionment, disorientation

(and, in a sense, 'catastrophe'), figures heavily in any theoretical enterprise. In this changed situation art has itself to define the scope of its own activity. Solutions are numerous and divergent: on one hand, there are signs of the rehabilitation of all kinds of values that were frustrated in previous decades of socialism, on the other hand (and more interestingly), completely new possibilities have opened for art. These are critically formed by a new relation towards both universality and more specific social and artistic demands. In this respect identity – always open to redefinition and reconsideration – proves to be neither self-evident nor given in advance (as in naive identifications with specific heritage models and elements).

I will now try to outline some basic characteristics of the present condition.

The context of Eastern European art in previous decades was determined by the repressive socialist system, to which it was uncritically related. Eastern socialist society prevented and frustrated any kind of effective modernism. Socialism tried persistently in its strategies of self-constitution (and through the purely ideological motivation of its ideas) to discredit modernism, or more precisely, modernist artistic forms. These were seen as 'degenerate' products of Western 'bourgeois cultural imperialism'. Additionally, if socialist realism (as a basic socialist art form) was a metaphor for ideological totalitarianism's method, promoting itself through propaganda, then it itself had to deny and exclude every characteristic and conceptual strategy of modern art in the most absolute terms.

The second characteristic, intrinsically connected with the suppression of modernism, is a kind of time delay: important achievements and works of art in the modernist context were recognised much more slowly in socialist countries. The legitimacy of contemporary art was not entirely denied, but certain works of art were not accepted until, through

Irwin, 'Capital', 1991, installation in the Clock Tower Gallery, New York

ABOVE: *Cosmokinetic Ballet,* The Praying Machine, *1993, Noordung; BELOW: New Collectivism, 1989, Städtische Kunsthalle, Düsseldorf, installation view*

specific historical appropriation, they were emptied of their 'dangerous' modernist potential and were thereby no longer regarded as confrontational in respect of socialist society. (We can recognise the same logic in relation to the very limited East European indigenous modernism of the avant-garde.)

Hence, if by definition postmodernism is always somehow related to modernism as its forerunner, then this relation in Eastern European 'postmodern' art is obviously problematic. Recent East European art is constituted in a completely different context, as a result of its relation to political totalitarianism, or, more precisely, social realism *in decay.* Eastern European art does not recognise itself in that relation to modernism and the problematic context of the commodity which is characteristic of Western postmodernism. Rather this recognition arises from the traumatic ideological field, which it reflects in different ways. Eastern European art in relation to its historical and political background managed to develop an alternative strategy, through the ironic appropriation and manipulation of the fundamental elements of totalitarianism. For example, the new conceptual (but socially and politically orientated) art in Russia seems to follow this kind of cynical logic and ironic strategy. Indeed, their important era of revolt, which began in the 70s and continued into the 80s, could never have been realised without this ironic, stylistic and cultural eclecticism. The use of political rhetoric and phraseology adopted and accentuated the language of direct totalitarian manipulation in order to break through it. At the same time this ironically transformed political sign formed a territory in which Eastern postmodernism could be distinguished from Western postmodernism and thereby establish an identity.

By categorically emphasising the immediately recognisable Eastern totalitarian experience, this idea also became an economic strategy in so far as its artifacts were rather different from other products on the art market. Apparently distant from the cynicism of Western consumerism and the vulgar object of consumer society, the artworks – playing with allusions to the socialist context – became commercial signs themselves. The need to be recognised as a part of a global artistic and informa-

tion system, in other words, brought a confrontation between social and political imagery and economic reality. Trading the images of totalitarian cultural codes serves to challenge the original socially critical purpose of these works. They are redefined as a sort of cover-up for establishing a role in the art market. And the art market is the very point where East and West really meet. The 'progressive and democratic' West is first of all that territory where the question of 'what does the East sell and what does the West buy?' arises. The East tries to be integrated in terms of mechanisms of commercial artistic exchange which did not exist or properly function in the countries of the Eastern Bloc. For the West, on the other hand, contemporary Eastern art is not so much attractive for its specific form and original demands as for the 'exotic', economically interesting dimension of its social context. (At this point we must note a similar logic in the current interest in 'war-subjects' from the former Yugoslavia.) It is precisely this 'interesting' quality that has to be focused on, along with its problematic consequences, because, paradoxically, through the changing context and art-market contacts with the West, it is becoming more and more threatened.

In the 90s, the revolutionary euphoria of the 80s has been replaced by the crisis of a post-totalitarian vacuum. The obsessive desire to get rid of manipulation has become a dominant strategy. It has lost its critical base and has started repeating and regenerated itself in a mere circle. The same thing is true in relation to the basic artistic idea of ironically mimicking the paintings of social realism or socialist social relations in general. So the real significance of the 90s consists in the attempt to go beyond this countercultural discourse based on irony. The conflict between ideology and counter-ideology, myth and de-mystification, is disappearing. The repressiveness of the state and old communist values does not exist any more, but a new general territory where art can act and function apart from its socially critical role, has not fully developed yet. That is why the current chaos of interpretations and possibilities and unclear future, is evidently a transitional period, with crisis of identity as its basic experience. But perhaps more than before, artists are forced to define their role on their own territory and no longer through the echo from the West. They are engaged in analysing situations and possibilities where their own distinctive artistic institutions can be established. The passage into the new shows the necessity for commercialisation, development of institutions, and different patterns of linkage between tendencies in the Eastern European context. This linkage has to establish new patterns of communication and exchange in relation to the position and functioning of art, precisely because in previous times, such positioning and functioning was severely inhibited by the lack of appropriate institutionalisation.

On the other hand, the broader dimension of art in society and the question of who art will be addressed to, are recurrent issues. Because of Eastern Europe's specific conditions and history, the political and social significance of products and their conflicting social context (or, more precisely, the interweaving of culture and ideology) are more pressing issues than purely artistic, aesthetic value. That is why direct communication between different tendencies is as necessary as the mere dissemination of art through media, galleries, magazines, etc. This modus vivendi of the collective and social (perhaps somewhat alien to Western experience) is necessarily connected with that dimension of art which involves the initiation of social changes. (In this respect, of course, it is noteworthy that art always played an important role in the recent political transformations in Eastern Europe). It is in this broad ideological context that we must understand events that happened in the spring of 1992 in Moscow. The Slovene group, NSK, prepared a special event called the *Irwin NSK Embassy*, as part of the *Apt Art International* project. This involved the exhibition of NSK artifacts and documents, constituted as representatives of a 'state' (ie as an NSK 'embassy') in a private apartment in Moscow, and the organisation of lectures and discussions which brought the social context of the ex-Soviet Union and ex-Yugoslavia into confrontation. The purpose/effect of this was to start a debate which in the future could play a role in developing interactions in the East European context. This project, in other words, is a basis for formulating new aspects of a specifically Eastern

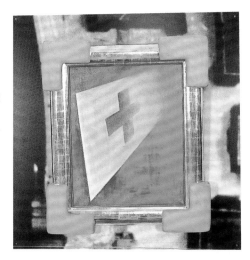

European identity. Its strategy was formally defined in the so-called 'Moscow Declaration'.

Of course, one cannot foresee the consequences of this idea in the future. Certainly, if it develops significantly it will encounter numerous problems. As noted earlier, specific changes are necessary – especially the concrete, practical problem of developing Eastern European art institutions, galleries, museums and the art-market . . . and other systems of interrelation. What is more difficult and problematic is the traumatic necessity of defining unitary identity which seems, paradoxically, more and more senseless in that it can have all possible senses. These encounters on a discursive level in Moscow actually embodied conflicting interpretations and visions. For example, the difference between conditions pertaining to art in Slovenia and in Russia is still enormous: Russian artists lived more directly in the centre of the totalitarian empire and were much more repressed than artists in Slovenia (or, more precisely, the former Yugoslavia). Because Slovenian art did not experience socialist mechanisms as deeply as the rest of the Eastern Bloc, it cannot, for the same reason, be entirely and simply located within the boundaries of the socialist-realism. Slovenia never created its own authentic tradition of socialist art (characteristic for example, of the former Soviet Union). On the contrary, Slovene art was always more concerned with problems more relevant to Western art and Western modernism. NSK is, in fact, the only artistic manifestation in Slovenia that relates itself to the totalitarian or socialist context, but even so, it uses completely different strategies and methods from those found in contemporary Russian art. For intellectuals and artists in Russia, there exists only one totalitarianism of meta-Stalinist discourse with its special social, political and cultural infrastructure; NSK is more diverse and interested in the multiplicity of domination and manipulation codes – hence, its members regard the period of socialism as only one of the historically important manifestations of totalitarian ideology. The ironical transformation of totalitarian signifiers was adopted in Soviet art as a means of transcending their ideological background. This characteristic type of ironic logic is not the strategy of NSK at all, and any resemblance is superficial. The NSK

Irwin, LZDS, 1990, 83.82x73.66cm

ABOVE: Emerik Bernard, Autumn, 1987, acrylic/montage, 194x350cm; CENTRE: Sergej Kapus, Metamorphosis I, 1988, acrylic on canvas, 200x140cm; BELOW: Andraž Šalamun, The Bull, 1986, acrylic on canvas, 290x400cm

strategy is to reveal different aspects of totalitarianism, in its complex, paradoxical, and universal mode. Reference to totalitarianism serves as a way of transforming ideology into *art object*.

NSK is a small artistic collective which was founded in 1983 as an organisation based on the idea of infringing the borders between ideology and art. It united the rock group Laibach (Laibach is the German name for Ljubljana), the artistic group Irwin and the Theatre of the Sisters of Scipio Nasica. (After an act of 'self-abolishment' in 1986, this theatre was reborn under the name of Red Pilot Cosmokinetic Theatre.) NSK today consists of other groups in addition: New Collectivism (designers), The Builders (architects), Retrovision (the video and film department) and the Department for Pure and Practical Philosophy. It was constituted as a collective artistic body with a basic rule for anonymity and collectivism. They appeared in the 80s as a media event with provocative ideological subject-matter, and caused a major appraisal in Slovene postmodern art.

NSK is aware of the fact that we are unable to escape from the ideological field. Their works consider the problem of domination and manipulative strategies in all forms – totalitarian (communist and national socialist), patriarchal, Christian . . . and challenge the manifold ideological phantasms that are circulating in both Western and Eastern culture and society. They open the political question of what role and status art has in relation to the functioning of ideological force, ie how art is able to manipulate, and how we are manipulated through art. Just as ideological symbols are used for the mere realisation of ideology, visual images in general prove to be the most efficient means of manipulation in our society. That is why NSK in their artistic practice refer not just to the same totalitarian visual material, but to the same communicative dimension and power of the images to point towards conflicting ideological situations.

The consequence of this (which may be even more important) is a demystifying of the ideological purity of modern art itself. NSK, through *overt* and complex ideological constructions in their paintings, point to the ideological loadedness and illusory innocence of modern art. They show that, far from being mutually

exclusive, art and ideology are intrinsically linked. What is unmasked here is not just the ideology of fascism, Nazism and socialism, which repress 'authentic' artistic impulses, but the ideological motivation of artistic form as a distinguishing trait of almost all Western art, and especially modernism.

The artists of the Irwin group employ direct quotations from totalitarian rhetoric and combine them with modern and postmodern references – not to criticise or deconstruct them but in order to affirm – in their words – that 'any art is given to manipulation except that which takes deliberately the language of manipulation'. NSK invert the strategy of aestheticising politics which is characteristic of propagandist totalitarian political regimes. In order to resist manipulation, they demand radical identification with domination systems – emphasising the political and ideological characteristic of every art. In their paraphrase of Goebels:

Politics is the greatest of all embracing art and we, who create the contemporary Slovene art understand ourselves as the politicians.

NSK's principle of total retro-eclecticism which appeared under the title 'retro-garde' could be easily understood (through its manipulation of given images and forms) as a postmodern methodological standard, as part of a specific tendency in contemporary art. This interpretation, however, should not be accepted completely.

Irwin uses themes that are straightforward historical quotations from Slovene and European tradition, images from high art and kitsch; avant-garde and Biedermeyer; Impressionism; Modernism; Third Reich; totalitarian rhetoric, national and communist symbols, crosses, trophies . . . but entirely transformed on the basis of a conceptual re-contextualisation. Retro-principle as the basic artistic strategy of NSK is not the chaotic excessive multitude which postmodern 'style' demands. It is experienced rather as historical fatality. NSK rejects the very idea of style and refers to Joseph Schillinger, who (in his book *The Mathematical Basis of Art*) divides the evolution of art into six stages, pre-aesthetic, traditional aesthetic, emotional aesthetic, rational aesthetic, post-aesthetic and the last stage – the retro method which is all aesthetic, or, more precisely, eclectic. It includes all previous manifestations of art and art forms. Retro principle is historical 're-make', an idea based on the premise that traumatic experiences from the past affecting the future (actual on all levels and territories of domination, socialism, Nazism . . . etc) can be overcome only by radical identification. This involves the direct repetition of totalitarian actions and images. Retro principle does not embody critical distance (and, indeed, rejects the fabrication of meaning as an ironical-critical position). Rather it confronts the art object with ideology through affirmatively articulated visual compositions. (Their accompanying texts and statements follow the same affirmatively eclectic logic.) NSK subverts totalitarian ideology by spectacular merging and absolute identification with its gestures, symbols and ideas of collective power. In 1984 the Irwin group proclaimed:

> The retro-principle advocates a constant changing of language, the switching from one form of art expression to another. It identically merges with art-history, selecting it together with culture as a whole as its field of activity. It will not renounce the accomplishment of modernism nor will it look for new set formulas: it is a way of thinking that advocates the process of assimilation.

The retro-principle leads to another social context, the continuity of Slovene past and the affirmation of its future cultural identity.

> Irwin dialectically elevate the historical experience of modernism through asserting the national culture, the triumph of collective spirit and through glorifying those characteristics of visual art which eclectic culture assimilates. Irwin re-establishes continuity of Slovene past and its traumatic experience as the only horizon of the future. Art represents retro-ritual in affirming eclecticism as a dynamic element inside the culture of the nation. The final aim of the functioning of the Irwin group is re-affirmation of Slovene culture in a monumental, spectacular way.

This eclectic motivation of affirming Slovene national culture is a re-valuation of Slovene art – which, like the art of every small nation, is necessarily eclectic. Their so-called 'organic eclecticism' outlines the belonging to a specific national territory where cultural identity is exemplified in the paradoxical empha-

sising of national identity. The basic necessity of Slovene eclecticism (formulated in the German sintagm 'Neue Slovenische Kunst' as the voluntary identification with 'foreign' influences) is, on the basis of retro-principle, transformed into a broader problem of originality in art itself. Through glorifying the eclectic characteristics which distinguish Slovene art, NSK tries to unmask another myth – the myth of originality which is, in terms of the concept of retro-gardism, ontologically impossible. Ideology (both in politics and art) does not create the original, but through repetition of its own images produces power.

The idea of national identity was realised in its broader sense in the exhibition 'Slovenian Athens' in 1991 in Ljubljana. *Slovenian Athens* is a painting by Irwin, composed as a monumental work of five pictures, representing motifs from five Slovenian regions, in the context of visual references to Magritte and Malevich, as well as Nazi and socio-realist symbols. They use, as their main reference, the picture *The Sower* by the Slovene impressionist painter Grohar. In the 'Slovenian Athens' exhibition this painting acted as a unifying link between the NSK project and a contribution that brought together 50 Yugoslav artists, with the basic idea of reconstructing and copying the work. *The Sower*, interpreted as a national icon, or, precisely, as a Heimatkunst allegory, served as a symbolic substitute for tradition, and, at the same time, a rejection of the original illusion of its impressionist ideological purity. The image of the sower functioned as an allegory of the artwork in its monumental form, raised to the status of an eternal ritual, and on that level identified as a national symbol.

NSK's retro-eclectic idea, then, was that the nation exists only if it is organised around national myth as the very point of its identity. However, whilst being theoretically consistent, in this practical context, the idea proved to be problematic. The exhibition permitted identifications on several levels and exposed a number of different and divergent approaches in relation to the fundamental idea. The general structure (the variations on the *Sower* theme) was based more on the 'contract' than on any solid belief or understanding where unitary definitions could be properly realised (as in other NSK artistic per-

Marko Jakše, Untitled, *1993*

13

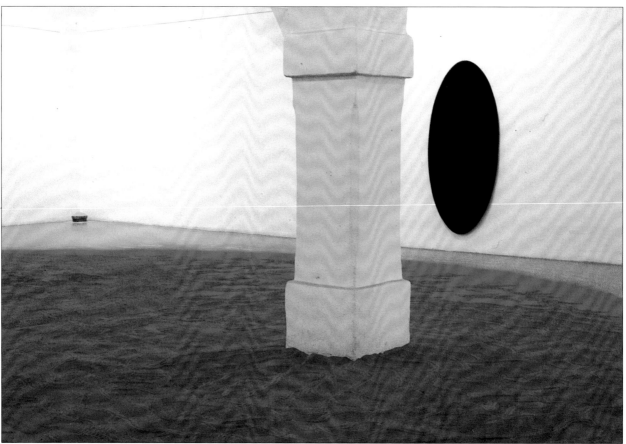

formances). But maybe the conceptual inaccuracy of the exhibition indirectly revealed the real territory of NSK practice and even affirmed its strategy.

NSK's is an art in the 'image of the state' (as they put it) which, through the repetition of the structures of society, revives the trauma of the avant-garde movement and philosophy. It does this by identifying with the stage of its assimilation in the system of totalitarian states, and confirms (by overturning the ideology in its 'mirror' stage in order to exceed it) that this state can only be that state as an object of art. If NSK as a 'suprematist' body with a specific social programme defines its collectivism with the framework of an autonomous state, then this state can only be constituted and installed in a real social and political space, as an artifact; not, in other words, as the real stage of broad social, political or cultural sanction, but only as an *exemplification*; as a complex idea of the state in a pure self-sufficient artistic manifestation. (It is perhaps from this point of view that we also have to understand the social action expressed in the 'Moscow Declaration'.) That is why the idea of the state is most explicitly or ideally realised in the status of the NSK theatre (the Theatre of the Sisters Scipio Nasica, or Red Pilot) as an image of a firm, geometrical, Utopian ('impossible') existence – an existence which can only save the 'enchantment' of its spectacular power in the form of art.

> The theatre is not an empty space, the theatre is the state. Therefore, it is an organisation which needs religion and a national myth to survive. However the aesthetic vision of the state is the vision of an impossible state, its components are stifled, lame and imbued with uneasiness.

As I have already mentioned, Slovene modernism was not wholly suppressed by the socialist-realist mainstream characteristic of other Eastern European countries, but at the same time it did not become highly developed. (As the Slovene critic T Brejc noted, Slovene modernism lacks three Cs – cubism, constructivism, conceptualism.) Slovene painters in the period between the wars were not especially interested in expressionistic tendencies nor preoccupied with formal issues. They tried to retain the 'mimetic' – symbolist tradition expressed in the style 'New Objectivity'. Even later on Slovene painters did not follow the

history of aesthetic modernism. Instead of privileging formality and exploring the limits of aesthetic self-referentiality, they sought to valorise the counter, anti-formalist (existentialist) impulse of modern art. Perhaps this 'impure' dimension of modernism was not consciously theorised in opposition to the formal purity of aesthetic modernism, maybe we can detect in it a certain conservative inability to understand modernism properly, and a desire to simply regard it at the level of cognitive coolness. On the other hand this characteristic existentialist position must be given its due. Its orientation towards ethical judgement rather than modernist epistemology enabled it to emphasise the close connection of existence and form. Tendencies such as 'psychotic emptiness', 'solitude' and 'darkness' expressed as transgressions of form, demanded a question of the ontological status of the modernist picture (Pregelj, Stupica).

A part of Slovene postmodernist art continues this same 'negative', 'dark' logic of art. Representatives of this are painters such as Huzjan, Gvardjančič, Kirbiš and E Bernard. (Bernard became the central figure in Slovene art of the 80s, with his tactile landscapes which reveal multiple meanings in well considered, huge palimpsest forms.) In the late 80s one of the basic questions asked was if it is still possible to create the conditions for establishing a 'new existentialist' art in the context of postmodernism. This would serve as an alternative to the 'exhausted' strategies of the new-image painting, nomadism, retro-gardism . . . But this possible strategy was very often only realised in terms of the repetition and affirmation of academic representational models.

At the same time the art inclined towards the New-Image movement found itself in a crisis. The early 80s witnessed works of art that could both by their form and their iconographical content be included in the widespread category of 'trans-avantgarde' or 'New Image Painting' regarded as a stylistic re-action to the demystifed modernism. Certain painters easily transformed their theoretical foundations from modernist to postmodernist structure (Gnamuš, Kapus, Gruden, Sušnik). In general, the 80s were marked by a transition to neoexpressionism, 'Bad Painting', trans-avantgarde etc . . . As a rejection of

OPPOSITE ABOVE: Marjetica Potrč, Torso and Landsape: Two Faces of the Lost Expectation, brick, felt, 198x300x400cm; BELOW: VSSD, Pure Eyewash, 1991, sand, pigment, wood; ABOVE: Bojan Gorenec, To the Non-Objective World, 1987, mixed media on wood, 141x141cm; OVERLEAF: VSSD, Look into the Eyes, Space-painting, Aperto, Venice Biennale 1993, detail

ideological, analytical conceptualism, the new expansion in art was in search of the possibility of a more direct mode of expression. The painters developed the phantasmagoric, allegorical and expressive aspects of painting. They travelled to America, Mexico, Berlin . . . and combined their international contents with references to Slovene tradition, politics, literature, history, as well as their subjective worlds and private mythologies . . . The nomadic transformation of previous styles and re-historicisation of modernism developed in a new pluralism of styles and 'autopoetics' (for example, humour and parody of Slak and Eric, The Mediterranean imagery of Šalamun and Marušič, eroticism of Krasovec . . .) But the original euphoria and belief in the expansion and renewed possibilities of the expressive image, soon subsided. Its theoretical base failed and it did not bring the 'liberation' that it was promising. It disappeared into privacy and the affirmation of subjective expression which proved (as everywhere else) to be a short-lived ecstasy.

The next generation of artists found themselves in more limited space and they resorted to more critically theoretical or personally engaged considerations of art. Specific orientations in Slovenian art of the 90s cannot be characterised in terms of some basic unitary style. It seems that because of the still inefficient and undynamic art market (which demands constant change and actually fetishises the idea of the new), artists in Slovenia are more orientated towards defining their work in a well considered theoretical discourse where everything needs to be explained and constituted in its specific status. (In Slovenia we absolutely lack artistic approaches that would reflect the commodity system or technological culture.) There are numerous metamorphoses of modernist method and references which in the new context of postmodern experience rediscover the self-identity of the picture or deconstruct basic dichotomies and question how, in the context of present reality, it is still possible to take pleasure in the contemplation of painted work. (Lenardič and Pogačar stress the physical dimensions of the painting. Zido explores the pictorial surface as a constant disappearing of the image . . . here we have to mention also painters such as Cervek, Gumilar,

Plotajs, Tusek, Fiser, Fistrič). On the other hand, a number of painters continue the figurative tradition. One might mention the ironic, illustrative images of Stančič and Varl, and complex figurative compositions of Kobal and Jakše, whose fantastic images, extraordinarily imaginative and painted with obsessive attention to detail, open bizarre psychological relations and meanings.

In the 80s sculpture regained an important position in Slovene art (in the work of Sambolec, Počivavsek, Vodopivec, Begič, Brdar, Barši, Bratuša, Zidar, Makše and Potrč). If we simplify and generalise, we could define the common theme in Slovene sculpture as an interest in the relation of the object to the body, ie *identifying* with the work in a total sense – involving the physical and tactile as well as the visual.

The sculptures of M Potrč in their physical attributes try to reflect the viewer's 'non-entirety' and prove that the viewer's look can no longer be the dominating 'master' and is, rather, continuously eliminated by the corporeal and optical constellations from which it is constantly emerging. This idea (based on Lacan's theory of the image and its chiastic intertwining of the eye and the gaze through which the subject is situated in a visual field) is expressed through the disappointment of the viewer's horizon of expectations. (For example, we are surprised when we suddenly notice that the rear side of the object does not coincide with expectations based on the frontal view.) A geometrical schema of the space (based on absolute points) transcends the status of the object as 'an appearance' and produces 'corporeality'.

Another attempt (this time in the painting) to impose a paradigm of a new vision proceeding from psychoanalytic theory is art by B Gorenec. He defines his pictures as the residence of the gaze (not the gaze of the beholder but that gaze which is intrinsic to the picture). His pictures try to be visual screens which can realise the paradoxical point of the visual, and of modernistic art in that they try to imitate the abstract picture and the possibility of abstraction itself. Gorenec's strategy is the opposite of that of customary modes of abstraction. He does not flatten the picture, his appeal rather lies in the question of how to achieve on canvas an illusionist, plastic rendering of the flattened image,

emerging and pulsating on the screen of imagination. Gorenec produces, in other words, a double vantage point – of painting, within the painting – flattened in its apparent illusionist aspect: 'I support the practice of painting which is able to recognise its internal dimension, its internal distances, and remain aloof towards itself, towards the Image in the Image.'

This difficult idea gravitates around the paradoxical dimension of the 'unpresentable' in painting. This needs to be stressed because it is probably the most important orientation in Slovene art and one which will require critical analysis in the future. That is why I would like to conclude this text with the idea, radically defined by an appeal to the impossible ethical stance embodied in the very name of the artistic group VSSD (Painter do you know your duty?). VSSD is one of the most important manifestations of the 90s in Slovenia. Their creations of 'total environments' oversaturated with images, and ornaments of organic and geometric forms, light installations multiple viewpoints, heaped materials, abundant details . . . try through the omnipresence of the visual to evoke exactly its opposition: the void, the lack, the 'blind' effect. The visual forced to excess stresses its extinction – a fullness twitching among deadened sensibilities, oscillates with emptiness. This obsession with visuality, which is an obsession with limits of the visual as an ultimate reference, becomes a duty to be performed. But where does its meaning really lie? A demand for visual 'terror' (in this context necessary, mythologised and sacred) adopts multiple strategies in order to regenerate attraction and desire. This kind of existence in art has brought painting, or more precisely the visual to the very edge – perhaps not just to be recognised there but rather to be recognised as the last attempt to endure in it.

THE MEDIA AND THE WAR

MARINA GRŽINIĆ

Nowadays I can write about 'the media' in general, and especially the medium of television, only in terms of the war, because I lived the ten-day war in Slovenia via television. At that time, June 1991, TV Slovenia was broadcasting 24 hours a day, and I had my TV set on continuously. Even when I managed to snatch an hour's sleep, the TV set stayed on, I just turned down the volume. It kept vigil for me, and I would wake regularly on the hour to hear how the war was 'progressing'. I turned my TV set off only when I ran into the cellar with my infant son to shelter from a potential air raid on Ljubljana by the Yugoslavian, then still the 'People's Army'. When the war in Slovenia stopped, rumours started spreading that all this bombing business had been staged to impress the foreign press, hoping to move the rest of the world to action, since Europe (it was said) would never really allow Ljubljana to be bombed. It was said that the more frequently the foreign press reported on running into air-raid shelters, the less likelihood there was of really being bombed. That was what we all kept repeating to ourselves (from Ljubljana to Vukovar to Sarajevo, Srebrenica and so on), that Western Europe, European peace movements, civil associations and last but not least, millions of TV viewers and other 'squatters' would remain dumbfounded at the direct TV pictures, the images of horror happening not somewhere in 'far-away Russia'[1] but in the heart of Europe.

Edmond Couchot[2] taught us that turning on the TV set actually means establishing a connection with the place of broadcasting and being literally (continually) present at the birth of the picture. The television picture materialises literally because of a short circuit between the place of transmission and the place of reception. But due to the speed of the transmission of the electronic signal, the television picture is practically simultaneous and we are not cognisant of the time lag. Thus we can with the aid of television, or more precisely the television video signal, establish a physical contact with the most traumatic events of our time.

I experienced this physical contact when watching on TV the 'Rumanian revolution', which, at least in the beginning, went 'live' into the world thanks to Belgrade. And it was supposedly thanks to television and to the millions of TV sets in the civilised world, in Europe and North America and not in the 'barbaric' East or far away in Africa or Asia, that that war ended on the same day. Due to technical electronic procedures, the TV viewer experiences events as though they are happening in the here and now. But relying on this almost physical contact between viewer and television, the contact which would rouse the world turned out to be, in the case of the events in Yugoslavia (Croatia and particularly Bosnia), an outstanding theoretical construct, and at the same time an erroneous empirical nexus. It may be true, as René Berger says,[3] that television has freed us from physically moving from one place to another and changed us into 'squatters' of satellite and cable television, but it has also saved us from much turmoil. On the threshold of the third millennium, information about war crimes in Bosnia and Herzegovina is, thanks to a certain short-circuit, not only simultaneously broadcast but also simultaneously tolerated in all parts of the world (at least until the war is really over and this is no longer merely wishful thinking).

The majority of European and world TV viewers know there is a war raging in Bosnia, and as long as this is documented in the media, we can suppose that they will not forget about Bosnia. Or maybe they will – precisely because it is always exposed and is so close and so far away at the same time! We are witnessing a paradox of television aesthetics. The aesthetics which offered us the co-ordinates of time and place as interminable electronic scan-

Gržinić/Smid, Bilocation, *1990, still from video*

19

ning, and the world as a simultaneous recording and transmission, have at the same time turned us away from remembering and establishing a balance between the past and the future in relation to the almost obsessive present of the television medium.

Even more, the conflict in the Balkans makes a mockery of the supposed omnipotence of the media.[4] The old notion that a counter effect can be achieved by showing horrifying visual material is no longer true. Each time it seems as though events in Bosnia have reached their peak, TV broadcasts greater horrors. And yet everyday TV reporting seems inconsistent with the logic of TV's informative-realistic effect, for it seems that the reports produce fiction, that the escalation of horrors (concentration camps, massacres, thousands of raped Muslim women) transforms fact into fiction. In 1987 Ernie Tee wrote in the catalogue for the exhibition 'Art for Television' that film was the medium of illusion, television the medium of reality and video the medium of metamorphoses,[5] but with the war in Bosnia television has become the medium of fiction, and, like fiction, it can perhaps present reality in the best way. As one of the standard codes of television narrative, sensationalism drew the short straw in this war. Daily reports from the battle zones are not sufficient coverage of the events in Bosnia, as if the media were frightened of offering a different slant on events, under the noses of the whole of Europe and America.

But maybe this war also shows us another internal process of the media and especially of society. This war can also be seen in another way. According to Peter Weibel we can think, for example, about this war in relation to the idea of what it means when we leave a historically defined position, which imitates – even through art – the natural world of our senses.[6] Our experience of place, position and so on depends on what we call natural interface. Body, for example, is a natural interface, and therefore we have a natural approach to space and time. Our interpretation of the media is experienced through the natural interfaces of our senses and is channeled and mediated by an ideology of naturality, neglecting the artificiality of the media. But the media of our time show us that we have the possibility of

an artificial interface, which is in fact the media. According to Weibel, therefore, McLuhan, when he was defining media as an extension of man, just missed in calling it an artificial extension.[7] And in this artificial media space we see that the basic concepts of how to construct space and time are examples of non naturality. The media world is dominated by non-identity or difference. The 'real' is replaced by virtual reality. Necessity is replaced by possibility or contingency.[8] So we have to think about 'reality' precisely in terms of its 'unreality' as a socially constructed fiction (the war in Bosnia television having become the medium of fiction). What we call reality, according to Jacques Lacan, constitutes itself against the background of bliss, bliss being an exclusion of the traumatic real.[9] What Lacan has in mind when he says that fantasy is the ultimate support of reality, is that reality stabilises itself only when some fantasy frame of a symbolic bliss forecloses the view into the abyss of the Real. Far from being a kind of dreamlike web, it prevents us from seeing reality as it effectively is. The point is that it shows us that reality itself is already a dreamlike construct. What this means is that the way in which the media function – for example television in relation to the war in Bosnia and Herzegovina – shows us all the dimensions of the so-called normal, active reality that is already ideologically, virtually constructed.

Moreover, when we insist on the consciousness of the TV viewer (relying on this almost physical contact between the viewer and television, the contact which will rouse the world!) maybe we count too much on the privileged position of the social as a positive. But what is showing us this changed, or other, position of television in relation to the war is, according to Arthur Kroker and David Cook, a precise rereading of Baudrillard, the collapse of the normalising, expanding, and positive cycle of the social into its opposite, an implosive and structural order of signs. The triumph of signifying culture means the eclipse of genuine social solidarities.[10] As I mentioned previously, information about war crimes in Bosnia and Herzegovina is, thanks to a certain short-circuit, not only simultaneously broadcast but also simultaneously tolerated in all parts of the world. So this war is not only changing the perception of the media as such, but also the perception of society. We face a kind of exteriorisation where strategies of normalisation are replaced by the simulation of the masses, where the hyperreality of culture indicates a great dissolution of the space of the social.[11]

In the old world of the social, according to Kroker and Cook, an emancipatory politics entailed the production of meaning: the control of individual and collective perspectives against a normalising society which sought to exclude its opposition. Society was constructed on the idea of the emancipatory subject who demanded a rightful inclusion in the contractual space of political economy.[12] On the contrary, Baudrillard's political analysis represents a radical departure from both the sociology of knowledge and theories of power/norm because he explores the brutal process of dehistoricisation and desocialisation which structure the new communicative order of signifying culture.[13] In *The Shadow of the Silent Majorities* Baudrillard provides three strategic hypotheses about the existence of the social only as having a murderous effect. The first hypothesis is that the social may only refer to the space of delusion, so the social has basically never existed. Second is the social as residuum and third the end of the 'perspective space of the social'.[14] The consequence, among other things, is that if the social is a simulation then the likely course of events (massacres, rapes etc) is a brutal de-simulation.

This refers also to two of the four great refusals of Jean Baudrillard concerning the classical, or perhaps it is better to say 'modernist', models of society's functioning; a rejection of the naturalistic discourse of the historical and a rupture with the normalising, and hence accumulative, conception of power.[15]

In such a 'new' world, television has the unreal existence of an imagist sign-system in which may be read the inverted and implosive logic of the cultural machine. Thus TV, according to Kroker and Cook, is not just a technical ensemble, a social apparatus, which implodes into society as the emblematic cultural form of a relational power. TV is not a mirror of society but just the reverse: it is society that is a mirror of television.[16] Television's major form of social cohesion is provided by the pseudo-solidarities of

electronic images whose public is, according to Baudrillard, the dark, silent mass of viewers who are never permitted to speak, and a media elite which is allowed to speak 'but which has nothing to say'. The explosion of information and implosion of meaning as the keynotes of mass communication, a massive circularity in which sender is receiver, an irreversible medium of communication without response – these are the strategic consequences of television as society.[17] Martin Jay in his latest book, *Force Field*,[18] refers to a similar idea in the Derridan coinage 'destinerrance', which suggests the impossibility of messages ever reaching their assigned destinations. The TV audience may be today the most pervasive type of social community, but if this is so, then it is anti-community or a social anti-matter, an electronic mall which privileges the psychological position of the voyeur (a society of the disembodied eye), and the cultural position of us as tourists in the society of the spectacle.[19] What else are Western Europe, European peace movements, civil associations and, last but not least, millions of TV viewers and other squatters but social anti-matter? Baudrillard's hypotheses about the media in connection with hyperreality and simulation, which were so ferociously criticised by 'serious' philosophers as to be a theoretical simulation – almost science fiction – seem, in the context of the war in ex-Yugoslavia, to have gained serious re-evaluation.

At least in my opinion, the most striking turn in the TV attitude to the war in ex-Yugoslavia, occurred about a year and a half ago, when the Serbs – or more precisely, the blood-thirsty Yugoslavian army under Serbian control – kidnapped Bosnian president Alija Izetbegovic, who was returning to Sarajevo after one of the innumerable international negotiating sessions. The only means of communication between the kidnapped president, the Yugoslavian army and the rest of the Bosnian presidency in occupied and already half-demolished Sarajevo, was by way of the then functional, though badly damaged, Sarajevo TV station. The talks and negotiations, the ultimatums and demands were carried out in their entirety and without censorship in front of the global TV auditorium before the international public got involved in the

affair and mediated Izetbegovic's release. All those involved could only communicate via TV telephone frequencies, and this while the TV station was broadcasting live. It was precisely at this point that TV – which was broadcasting the image of a competent newsreader mediating between generals, the president and the presidency – paradoxically was transformed into radio and became the medium of drama and information, *par excellence*. With this turnaround television really functioned in the way in which theorists supposed it would, dumbfounding TV audiences in the broadest sense of the word and forcing them into action.

Nevertheless, the edge of the general media situation is not ecstasy and decay but the addiction of hyper-primitivism and hyper-imaging. Baudrillard described in *Simulacres et Simulation* the current mood: 'Melancholy is the quality inherent in the mode of disappearance of meaning, in the mode of volatilisation of meaning in operational systems. And we are all melancholic.'[20] Melancholia is thus, Jay suggests, not simply an illness but a kind of permanent dimension of the human condition. A great number of authors distinguish between melancholia and mourning, which are not specific states of mind but two different attitudes towards the world. Referring to Freud's text 'Mania and Mourning' from 1917, Jay pointed out that the refusal to test reality can still help us to make sense of the distinction between mourning and melancholy, for it is precisely the ability to do so that distinguishes the former from the latter.[21] Melancholy, with its manic depressive symptoms, means the inability to mourn or to reflect reality. Melancholy, wrote Jay, 'seems to follow the logic of what Freud calls elsewhere disavowal or foreclosure in which inassimilable material seems to be cast out of the psyche and reappears in the realm of a hallucinatory 'real'. Instead of being able to consciously identify what actually has been lost, he or she remains caught in a perpetually unsubstantiated dialectic or self-punishing fear and manic denial.[22] Mourning is important because it allows us the strategic emotional process of reflexivity which allows us to survive this transitional period. On the other hand, mourning as a complete working through of lost material is itself a Utopian myth. The hope of finding a means to completely transcend

the repetition and displacement characteristic of apocalyptic melancholia is necessarily doomed to failure.[23]

The paradigm of melancholy can be useful for working through the mode of how (Western) Europe and its civil institutions deal with the war in the ex-Yugoslavian territory, especially in Bosnia and Herzegovina. This specific 'mode' can be interpreted in similar terms 'like the object which is confronted by the impossibility of conscious working through it'. The questions that such a hypothesis raises are obvious: what is the object (or objects) whose loss cannot be confronted, and why does it remain so resolutely disavowed, so resistant to a conscious working through?[24] So, we are trying to locate a specific historical trauma that resists the mourning process. According to Jay:

The monotheistic religions like Judaism and Christianity sought to replace their mother-goddess predecessors with a stern patriarchal deity, then perhaps the lost object can be understood, in a sense maternal. Mourning would mean working through the loss produced by the archaic mother's disappearance. An inability to renounce the regressive desire to reunite with the mother in a fantasy of recaptured plenitude, when accompanied by the unconscious self-reproach that her death was covertly desired, would result in melancholia instead.[25]

It seems that 'civilised' Christian Europe is programmed by the symbolism to reunite with the remaining Christian parts, constantly fortified and destabilised by the Muslim 'other'. This was also formulated simply by Tomaz Mastnak:

European peace has never parted from war. The way of freeing Europe from wars was to export them to non-European territories, or to the margins of Europe. Moreover, the idea of European unity is intimately connected to the idea of war, or a real war, against an enemy from without, and as a rule that enemy is the Muslim. The Muslim is the symbolic enemy of Europe, and I do not believe that it is by accident that Euro-Serbian policy has made Muslims out of the Bosnians. The image of the warring Muslim invokes both the Urangst of the Christian, cultured, and civilised West, and the

Gržinić/Smid, Three Sisters, *1992, stills from video*

more recent spectre haunting Western politicians and intellectuals, that of 'Islamic fundamentalism'. The Slavs, it is true, are only second-class, or potential, Europeans, but Muslims simply do not belong to Europe. That is why it is assumed that the Bosnians are not Slavs.[26]

The Muslim reality in Europe, if I may cynically paraphrase Derrida, is understood both as poison and as cure.

In the end, the medium of video, or more precisely video art works, in relation to the war. (I personally have made video art in collaboration with the Slovenian video artist Aina Smid for more than a decade.)

Only one topic seems to dominate the Slovenian art production of the 80s and in the 90s, and in a more general way the art production of what is called the East European paradigm, and that is history. This is no yearning for the past, though, rather a desire to retake possession of our own history. All the major moves in the art system can be measured by the dissection and rebuilding of that very history, supplemented with ineffable thoughts, images and facts. Yet in the Slovene 'post-war' period (which took place in June 1991 against the tanks of the Yugoslav government), history has begun to play a starring role in art and in culture, not only as a means of retaking possession of the history of socialism, deformed as it was, but also in order to reject the blind retaliation, nationalism and racism that can rise out of the 'ruins of war'.

The video medium, especially video art (because of its cheaper production and manipulation bases in comparison with film and television productions) may be developing a specific 'viewer', enabling us to read history, to see through the surface of the image, and perhaps to 'perceive' the future. In a more general sense, the future of film and documentary imagery lies in the viewpoint of video (or more exactly of digital computers). Through an electronic and digital process of 'incrustation', in fact, a concrete destiny for television, film and documentary material is being realised. The video *Bilocation* (1990) by Gržinić/Smid, which suggests the residence of the body and soul in two different places at the same time – an appropriate delineation of the video process as such – describes Kosovo's history of blood and hell; this region in the south of

Serbia is tormented by national disorders and torn apart by the conflict between the Albanians and Serbs who live there. Original documentary material about the 'Civil War' in Kosovo made by TV Slovenia was juxtaposed with synthetic video images, images disintegrated and reconstructed through optical and digital technology. In the videos *The Sower* (1991) and *Three Sisters* (1992), both by Gržinić/Smid, the documentary material from the war in Slovenia and Croatia was used to compose a story based on the possibility of intertwining the inner and the outer worlds. The video work *The Sower* is a story about the political and mythical universe of Slovenian art and culture in 1991. The documentary material used in the video is taken from the ten-day war in Slovenia in June and July 1991. Art and its political background is discussed here, and conversely, the political chaos in ex-Yugoslavia is framed by art.

The video *Three Sisters* presents a different reading of the classic Chekhov play, in a changed political and artistic context. The video identifies with the Zeitgeist of war in Croatia at the beginning of the 90s. The digitalised documentary shots of the war in Croatia, incrusted with scrupulously constructed fictional material, produce mental and visual hybrids. Instead of simply identifying with a documentary about our present situation, the irrational and complex structures of electronic and digital processes offer us paradoxes and non-linear editing. The peace conferences to stop the war in Bosnia and Herzegovina today seem to be constructed with equal skill. The slow-motion tracking of the camera along the electronic edges of the conference tables ('There will be no more fundamental reason for shelling') creates empathy and anxiety where apathy reigns. The video can be also understood as an attempt to talk about communism falling apart, about racism and nationalism, and about a new political machinery of market capitalism, exemplified by our remaking of one of the classical Benetton commercials. It also explores the relationship between Chekhov and Eisenstein, (particularly *Battleship Potemkin*), and between Chekhov and De Palma (particularly the film *The Untouchables*).

The re-using of documentary video and television material (often non-stylised and non-narrative) enables us also to compare the national mass-media interpretations of those same events and to locate the responsibility for particular versions of history. The video work *Labyrinth* (1993) by Gržinić/Smid juxtaposed the artificially constructed surrealist imagery of René Magritte (*The Eternal Evidence*, *The Sorcerer*, *Young Girl Eating a Bird*, *The Heart of the Matter*, *The Lovers* etc) with documentary shots of the camps where Bosnian refugees, mostly Muslims, live in Ljubljana. The video process of 'reappropriation' – the recycling of different histories and cultures – resulted in a multi-cultural, hybrid aesthetic condition. The effect of these processes is akin to an 'interior-culturalism' with

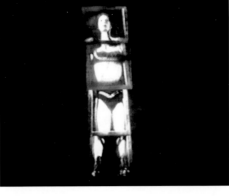

international influence and resonances. The video image presents a persistent searching for the condensed point which is simultaneously the past and the present. It constitutes the deconstruction of time, based on memory and the balance between the past and the future. The result of such procedures is the development of an imagery which refers neither to the past nor to the present, but to a potential time, somewhere between certainty and potentiality. That is why one can define video art as providing an alternative history, which gathers the names and the faces of forgotten or discarded cultures, redefining its place inside a contemporary construction of power relations.

Notes

1 What was a cynical allegory in December 1992 and January 1993, when a part of this text was written, in October 1993, when I am revising the text seems a frightening reality.

2 Cf Edmond Couchot, 'La question du temps dans les techniques électroniques et numériques de l'image', in *3e Semaine Internationale de Video* (Saint-Gervais Genève, 1989), pp19-21.

3 Cf René Berger, 'Entre magie et voyance', in *3e Semaine Internationale de Video*, pp11-14.

4 Cf the texts by Melita Zajc about television aesthetics in the Slovenian weekly magazine *Mladina*, Ljubljana, 1992/93.

5 Ernie Tee, 'The Irreality of Dance', in Kathy Rae Huffman and Dorine Mignot (eds), *The Arts for Television*, The Museum of Contemporary Art, Los Angeles and Stedelijk Museum, Amsterdam, 1987, p62.

6 Cf Peter Weibel, 'Ways of Contextualisation or The Exhibition as a Discrete Machine', in Ine Gevers (ed), *Place, Position, Presentation Public*, Jan van Eyck Akademie and De Balie, Maastricht and Amsterdam, 1993, p225.

7 Ibid, p225.

8 Ibid, p228.

9 Ibid, p230.

10 Cf Arthur Kroker and David Cook, *The Postmodern Scene, Excremental Culture and Hyper-Aesthetics*, St Martin's Press, New York, 1986, pp172-73.

11 Cf Jean Baudrillard, *In the Shadow of the Silent Majorities*, Jean Baudrillard and Semiotext(e), New York, 1983, pp3-4.

12 Kroker and Cook, op cit, p175.

13 Ibid, p175.

14 Cf Jean Baudrillard, *In the Shadow of the Silent Majorities,* in Kroker and Cook, pp173-174.

15 Cf Kroker and Cook, op cit, p171.

16 Ibid, p268.

17 Ibid, op cit, p176.

18 Cf Martin Jay, *Force Fields*, Routledge, New York and London, 1993.

19 Kroker and Cook, op cit, p274.

20 Jean Baudrillard, 'Sur le nihilisme', *Simulacres et Simulation*, Editions Galilée, Paris, 1981, p234 in Martin Jay, 'The Apocalyptic Imagination and the Inability to Mourn', in *Force Fields*, pp84-99.

21 Martin Jay, 'The Apocalyptic Imagination and the Inability to Mourn', op cit, p90.

22 Ibid, p93.

23 Ibid, p97.

24 Ibid, p94.

25 Ibid, p94.

Gržinić/Smid, Labyrinth, *1993, stills from video*

CZECH ART TODAY

ON THE DEATH OF CZECH CULTURE
Ian Mckay

In his catalogue essay to the recent exhibition at Manchester City Art Gallery, 'Europe Without Walls: Art, Posters and Revolution 1989-93', exhibition organiser for the office of the Czech president, Tomáš Pospiszyl, outlined a fundamental problem in addressing the arts of his country. The language problem that continues to blight an understanding of Czech art is, for Pospiszyl, rooted in what he claims to be 'the English reticence to express truly deep feelings and thoughts'.[1]

I want to show here just how deep-rooted this problem may be, but in examining current art from the Czech and Slovak Republic, I also hope to show that the internationalist trends of a Western art 'system' are bringing about a catastrophe for that art – far greater perhaps than that which occurred under communism.

This, of course, is a sweeping statement, but already there is evidence on which to argue that the internationalising force that drives that art system is destroying the very fabric of a fragile Czech culture.

My own reports on art from Czechoslovakia began with an article published in *Artscribe* in 1989;[2] It was a time of optimism and great energy in the country. The prospects looked good. By 1992, however, the situation had deteriorated to such a point that freelance journalist Caroline Juler was able to report in *Art Monthly*[3] that artists were by then suffering from a suspicious viewing public that shunned them. Dealers were suffering from that same public's response to the art they showed and the only successful dealer was one who operated a ruthless business that continued to hurt the small artist.[4] 'Unlike the bad old days of communism,' said Juler, 'people are not buying contemporary art . . . Politically, socially and economically, things are changing every day, while Czechoslovaks have to ditch one ethos for living and replace it with another which has no clear rules.

No wonder that few people feel confident enough to risk splashing out on original oils, collages and sculpture as they would once have done.'

This situation was exactly that which I and others had prophesied in the heady days of the *velvet revolution* band-wagon-jumping of 1989. Elsewhere I had warned repeatedly[5] that if the then current enthusiasm for the internationalising of Czech art was to continue without caution, Czechoslovak artists would experience great hardship. In short, the Czech art world was biting off more than it could chew. With the Western art market in the depths of the worst recession the art (business) world had seen, an entire system of dealership and art enterprise was being exported; a system which at home was already bankrupting dealers of repute.

In understanding the current situation for Czech art, we must first look back to 1989 and the move to internationalise its art assets. So many artists were then accepting the new painterly call to order that in Britain had been made by the Royal Academy of Arts with the *New Spirit in Painting* show of 1981. Artists such as Petr Nikl, Daniel Jurkovic and Jaroslav Róna were being heralded as the forebears of a Czech renaissance. In Prague the critic Pavel Zadrazil (echoing a Western belief in neo-expressionism expressed by Christos Joachimides, Norman Rosenthal and Nicholas Serota, amongst others)[6] was claiming that 'new elements of spiritual alliance are being accepted and then questioned and updated by the creation of new levels where the old iconography will not do. It is possible to speak about the reinstatement of myth, faith and mystery in the form of a new world mythology.'[7]

Róna himself was becoming increasingly interested in his nation's mythic history. Indeed when I first attempted to make contact with him, calling his studio in the old Jewish Cemetery in Prague, his answer-phone carried a message

Miloš Šejn, Waterfall – Maple Brook in the Giant Mountains, *1987*

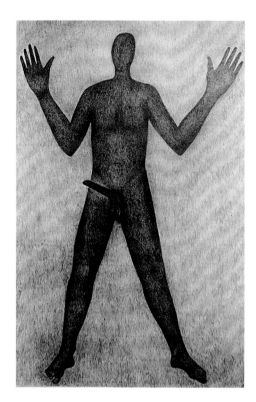

ABOVE: Petr Nikl, Birth of an Animal, 1987, oil on canvas; CENTRE: Jaroslav Róna, Sleeping Boy, 1988, wax and tempera on canvas, 100x160cm; BELOW: Petr Jochmann, Untitled, 1991

from the Golem of the city, (golem means 'unformed' in Hebrew) an artificial man who is formed from the earth and brought to life by the elements of fire, water and air. Róna and Nikl's paintings in particular, it seemed to me, drew heavily on the art and design found in the Prague National Museum. Argilite sculptures of the second century BC or Bohemian Romanesque all appeared to be precursors of the artists' new found symbolism.

Other Czech artists such as Petr Jochmann had meanwhile begun to concretise their earlier metaphysical, quasi-abstracted landscapes and embrace a new, overtly figurative practice. The abstraction of elder statesmen of Czechoslovak art such as Bostik and Urbasek was giving way to a new figurative voice in the work of younger artists many of whom were forming into groups whose primary function was to challenge the platitudes of the Artists' Union. Above all what was happening was a self-conscious jettisoning of late-modernist conceptual concerns by the younger generation.

James Aulich, co-selector of the Manchester City Art Gallery exhibition and senior lecturer in the History of Art at Manchester Metropolitan University, rightly insists that such attention to the past and (in the work of those mentioned above) to the figurative tradition, is 'one of the noted effects of the revolution . . . a kind of catching up'.[8] In a text published by artists born between 1950 and 1970,[9] the artists themselves bear this out by saying that 'after several decades of cultural destruction we have put together belated information on our own culture of our own time, in order to settle the debts incurred by a social system which was both unjust and against nature.'

Aulich goes on to quote Vaclav Havel when he says,[10] 'Nations are now remembering their ancient achievements and their ancient suffering, their ancient suppressors and their allies, their ancient statehood and their former borders, their traditional animosities and affinities – in short, they are suddenly recalling a history that, until recently, had been carefully concealed and misrepresented.'

As Havel claimed, nothing may have been forgotten, but already there is a new, more insidious regime, which is burying the very truths unearthed by the

likes of Róna, Jochmann and Nikl only four or five years ago. It is the trend towards internationalism that has for so long been the blight of Western art. Something similar happened in Hungary in the 1890s just as it is happening today in the Czech and Slovak Republics, and there is much that could be learned from that history.

1896 marked the one thousandth anniversary of the arrival of the Magyar people to Hungary. The anniversary was to be an unprecedented display of national prosperity across all of the country, embodying a national identity, enhanced by all who were involved in the Hungarian cultural industry. In a sense the revolution of 1989 in Czechoslovakia carried with it similar aspirations. Culturally, Hungary wished to reveal itself as a potent force which owed nothing to Vienna, its sister city which until then had overshadowed Budapest. Painters, sculptors, designers and architects joined forces in a brave attempt to identify their National History.

It was not an easy task, for as historian Lajos Németh recalls, unlike Austria, 'Hungary with no middle-class tradition, had not only to shape the present and the future, but also to *create* a comprehensible past'.[11] We would do well to remember here that Czechoslovakia itself was a country that had only become such in 1918.

The emergence of modern Hungary would be a painful and prolonged re-birth as over a ten-year period artists were encouraged to deal with themes that helped the ideologists with 'the ennobling of virtue', establishing middle-class sensibilities in the hearts of a people that, as Németh has said, 'simply drank, played cards and meddled in politics in a slogan saturated atmosphere'. Slowly, very slowly, the Hungarian style began to take shape.

Nevertheless, what had been intended as a move which would ensure Hungary's prominence as a centre of artistic excellence in Europe, back-fired as she began stylistically to fall behind other centres such as Paris, Munich, and the rival, Vienna – cities that her artists had emigrated to in order to work ostensibly with an international style, freed from the provincialist interests of their government.

The art that those Hungarian artists brought back with them upon the Hungarian call to order was not an authentic

Hungarian art but an art informed by European Symbolism, Impressionism, Art Nouveau and Jugendstil. Such was true of emigré artists returning to Czechoslovakia in 1989 too. Their view of the country had become 'distorted' through the passing of time and ultimately through contact with a late-modernist endeavour in the West. Through Western eyes, however, they had been seen as the torchbearers of their nation's culture.

In the mid 80s if you asked anybody about 'Czech art', they would invariably direct you to a gallery – such as the Flaxman in London's East End – which dealt with a few emigré Czechs. Emigré Czech art *was* Czech art to the West. If one persisted, calls would be made and a path unravel itself, usually ending at the doors of the BBC World Service at 10.00pm on a Sunday night. It was in this way that I first got hold of exhibition catalogues from Czechoslovakia containing essays and images by Czech critics and artists still living in the country. For the most part, however, the press tended to see Czech art as that which was being produced in Western Europe or in the States. To be able to market art in terms of the 'iron curtain factor', did not worry dealers either, even if the artist was living happily in Hampstead, Highgate or Houston.

In 1989 these exiles who, in Aulich's words, 'had not thought it wise to return to their countries of origin, did so for the first time in 50 years. But with so much, and so little, to say, nothing could fill the lifetime of experience that divided them from their pasts and their countries from their histories.'[12]

The photographer Yuri Dojc did not return to live. He still resides in North America. The cultural icons of his adopted country evince the way in which so many emigré Czechs became enmeshed in the surreal technologies of a foreign culture, in part as a *reaction to* the regime which they left behind them. Nevertheless, his work is still marketed here in England in terms of its 'Czechness'.[13] Jana Sterbak is another, living in Canada, who more successfully than Dojc has kept her 'Czech spirit' alive. The Golem, for instance, was present in her sculptural installation featured at the Liverpool Tate Gallery recently.[14] The all-pervading existential angst so often attributed to Kafka is a primary theme of her work and a meta-

morphosis of sorts recurs again and again in her projects dealing with heavy metals and gasses. Those artists that did return to Czechoslovakia, as free-lance critic Dr Marcela Pánková has outlined, took with them 'their artistic and human experiences. As a consequence many questions relating to foreign influences and national identity . . . arise in connection with their reappearance on the domestic art scene.'[15]

It was just such a dilemma that faced Hungary in 1896; in constructing an intelligible history from the bloated underbelly of the Austro-Hungarian Empire, and furthermore drawing on the experiences of artists already embedded in the avant-garde of Munich or Paris, Hungary herself became nothing more than a cheap pastiche of the cultural autonomy she had sought.

If the same is happening in the Czech and Slovak republics today, then we are all to blame here in the West for fostering a similar optimism in post-1989 Czechoslovakia. The newsworthiness of art journalist Philip Vann's serialisation 'Art In Czechoslovakia' in *Artist's and Illustrator's Magazine*[16] for instance, like my own writing on the subject for numerous other art magazines, was at the time simply seen as good copy by our editors. Even the *Economist* was running reviews of Czech art in order to keep up with developments in the East being reported in its financial section. It all added spice to what in Britain was becoming a more and more complacent art press.

It remains a fact that we did not, and could not, fully understand what was happening. As Aulich goes on to highlight, it is necessary for Westerners to own the inadequacies of their powers of comprehension when interrogating the issues of the Czechoslovak revolution. 'By 1992,' he says, 'many [Czechoslovaks] were bored or irritated by the naivety of Westerners, like myself, who marvelled at the historical enormity of the events that had taken place.'[17]

The Czechs found hope in our interest initially because they realised what was needed was international media coverage in order to maximise the effects of their action in challenging the State and in terms of art, its Artists' Union. But that was quite a different thing to internationalising their art. The British failed a crucial test in understanding Czech art as they have in

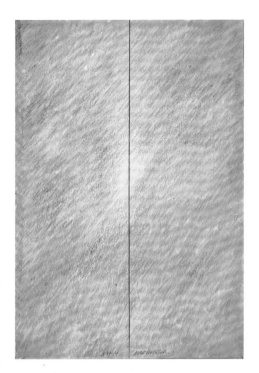

ABOVE: Milos Urbasec, Untitled, *1984; CENTRE: Yuri Dojc,* Untitled, *1993; BELOW: Yuri Dojc,* Untitled, *1993*

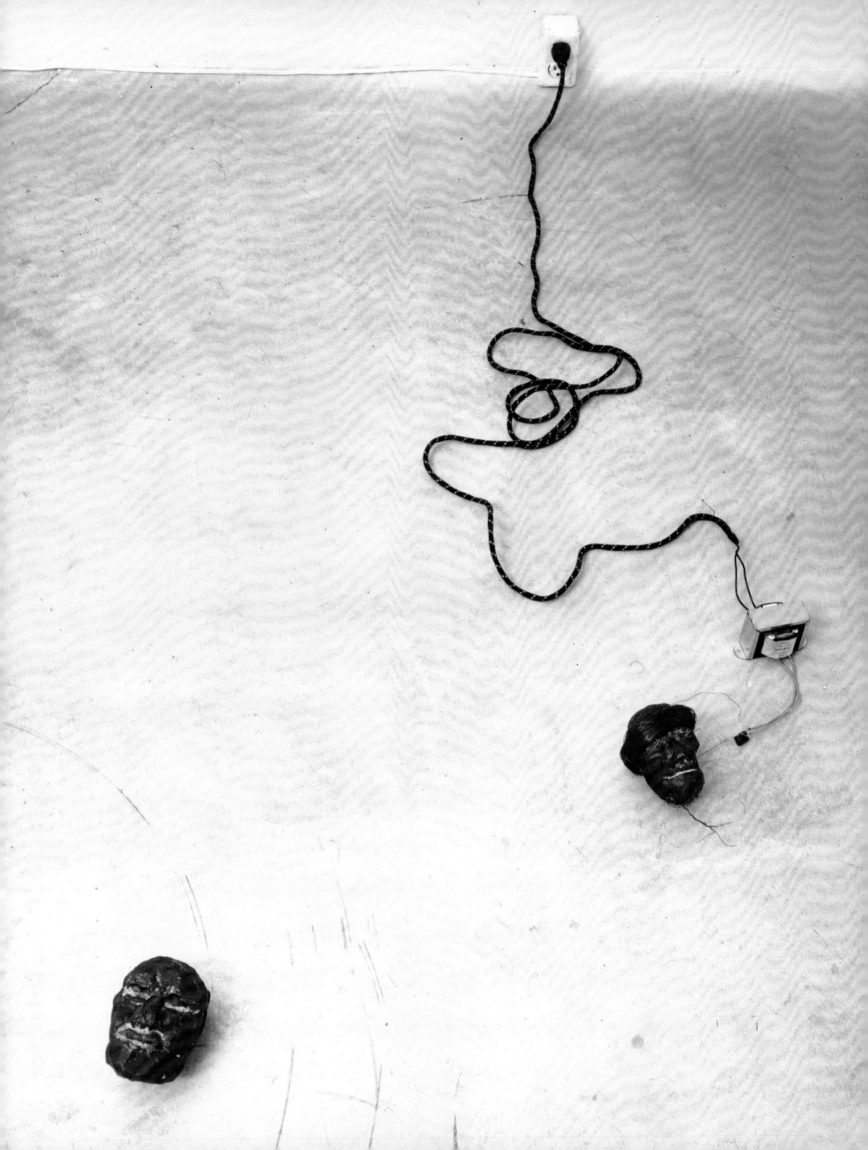

understanding the arts of all Eastern Bloc countries. In turn the Czechs failed to envisage fully the way that their art and new-found histories could be incorporated into the international style of cultural pluralism.

Another facet of the Western system from which the Czechs had been sheltered was the cultural imperialism of the dealer system itself. In 1992 I interviewed Dr Agnes Husslein of Sotheby's, Vienna, who was then organising symposia such as that held in Budapest during 1991. The intention of the Sotheby's symposia was to 'inform dealers of how to "internationalise" their art', she claimed.

Brett Gorvy, features editor of the *Antique Collector* magazine, meanwhile claimed that similar moves in the Soviet Union had previously 'totally screwed up the Moscow art market'. Aulich is adamant that such symposia, which free art of ideology and history, are also guilty of 'cleansing it, as it were, for the international market'. Whilst the Czechs were rooting out their cultural and ideological history, searching for a tangible identity which could cosset them in the post-revolution years, Western dealers were already muscling in with a view to making a fast buck off the back of the revolution. Even the emigré Hungarian dealer Kalman told me, 'Who knows what's going to be popping up in attics and closets all over Hungary?'

What has happened in Czechoslovakia during the last four years is that the need for an international readership got lumped in with the need for hard currency following the revolution. Artists and dealers who had built relationships with the Western press and Western dealers, continued to attract attention by naively marketing their art abroad. In November 1989 one academic at Prague's Museum of Arts and Antiquities had informed me, 'the basic duty towards knowledge of Czech art is that it needs to be recognised as an authentic part of modern European art, valued and worthy of being recognised as such, and in turn the duty of the Czech artist would be to present it in its complete scope to the European society'.

The art press were not interested in 'the complete scope' however. My article for *Artscribe* had been tailored to fit the emerging style of the magazine as a champion of 'Neo-Geo' trends of the late 80s by one of the many editors that

worked for the magazine before its demise. Good quality reproductions of Róna and Nikl's images were cut from the text that dealt with the emerging figurative art from Prague, and instead, the magazine used the sparse, hostile minimalism of Milos Sejn to create a view of a bleak Eastern Europe devoid of spiritual or traditional aesthetic values.

The emergence of authentic Czech art was for the most part a media exercise, and the Czechs may be forgiven for not seeing it coming. Czech photographer Pavel Stecha, found that the Western media's insatiable appetite for stereotypical imagery of civil unrest could provide him with a supply of photographic paper which in Prague was in short supply. In January 1990 he wrote enclosing photographs to run with an article. 'I am glad and happy,' he said, 'and just now very inside the situation emotionally . . . I'm run out of Kodak 3200. If you could arrange some it would be great.' Little did he see that what he described as 'our revolution, our future, our hopes' were being shaped to mean something quite different for a Western readership.

As Stecha saw it he was 'exporting truth'. What he did not, indeed could not, envisage was that for the most part, Western editors cared little for the integrity of the imagery as long as it 'looked right'. Everybody in the West knew that the Western art world cared little for truth. Art was treated by many that held the pursestrings as an expendable commodity and their relationship to it was vulgar to say the least. If Stecha's naive 'honesty' – his picture of students offering flowers to riot police in Prague – was ever a success, it could only be as an indictment of our own corruption.

The reason for such misunderstandings are fundamentally rooted in that language barrier, highlighted in Pospiszyl's essay mentioned above.

The Czechs in 1989 functioned in a culture which despite the ravages of communism – perhaps as a result – was rooted in the idea of an intelligentsia which remained intact. As they saw it, the intelligentsia was responsible for leading them out of the quicksand of state intervention in all aspects of their lives. One Czech friend found it impossible to believe that in Britain we do not operate in the certainty of such an intellectual culture. The very word 'intelligentsia', which first emerged in

OPPOSITE: Jana Sterbak, I can hear you think (Dedicated to Stephen Hawking), *1984-85, iron, copper wire, transformer, magnetic field and electrical cord; Miloš Šejn, ABOVE:* Vestiges of Iron, *1987, found pigment on untextured textile, 192x288x96cm; BELOW:* World within a World: Zebin Hill, late spring, *1987, landscape work, paper*

ABOVE: *Pavel Stecha*, November 17, 1989; BELOW: *Vaclavske Namesti*, November 23, 1989, Prague

Russia in the 1860s, does not feature as a plural form of the academic intellectual in Britain and America, let alone enjoy common currency in the minds of the general public.

Psychologist Liam Hudson has shown how intellectuals are removed from the everyday lives of the people of this country in a way that they were not in Czechoslovakia. 'Even when talking about moral issues,' says Hudson of Oxford in the 50s, 'the Oxford philosophers used trivial examples; in fact, there seemed some tacit competition to achieve the greatest possible triviality . . . they discussed hypothetical men on hypothetical islands, never real gas chambers, real Jews.'[18] This inherent 'Philistinism', as Hudson sees it, has led (at least) British academics into a verbal destructiveness that is 'both cheap and facile'.

Sheltered from such a cynicism, the likes of Stecha failed to understand that the intelligentsia is only potent so long as it has a focus; in the case of Czechoslovakia, the State itself. In overthrowing the State, Czechoslovakia overthrew the very focus through which their engagé criticism functioned. At the time the *Economist* was running a piece about the new president, Vaclav Havel, entertaining Frank Zappa at Hradcany Castle! As Germaine Greer insisted in *Oz* way back in 1969 however,

> Zappa may enjoy his artistic and other sorts of integrity, but he will never make a contribution to the revolution of sensibility which is the pre-requisite of political revolution . . . The rock revolution failed because it was corrupted. It was incorporated in the capitalist system which has power to absorb and exploit all tendencies including the tendencies towards its overthrow.[19]

Was that not what was happening to Czech art, I wondered? In their search for a cultural identity, Czech artists relied too heavily on the Western art system. They incorporated too much of the internationalist trends of Western art for their own ever to be fully conceived as part of their unique cultural history. The Czech art world is now emerging from the years under communist rule only to embrace a pluralist European aesthetic that is corrupt and bland.

Take for instance Milan Knížák's *Czech Landscape No 1*, 1990, which resembles so much art that has been fashionable in Western Europe for some time. As Aulich claims, Knížák addresses the significance of folk tradition and examines the hold that it maintains for dissident intellectuals such as Vaclav Havel. 'Havel,' says Aulich, 'like many others, found himself in an uncritical relationship to national traditions simply out of the desire to remain loyal to his origins.'[20] What is presented by the artist therefore, is an incongruity which no doubt underlies a contemporary truth for the Czech people, but in terms of a broader Czech tradition that Havel himself defends, Knížák's statement is both banal and vacuous. It corresponds well to the visual incongruity of much Western art that presents the detritus of everyday life with the intellectual idea as its root stimulus. In a society where art's primary function is to stimulate contemporary discourse owing to its suppression in the slogan-saturated broader sphere, the intellectual idea may well be enough to sustain its integrity. In a Prague that is liberated from the grip of totalitarianism, such ideas do not make great art. The function of art in the Czech and Slovak Republics has changed.

What Knížák's art reflects, but does not comment on in an intelligible way, is an emerging culture that is the product now of 'a development-hungry government driven by monetary policies'.[21] In a society in which 'posters are for Coca-Cola and art pursues the banality of the market and the platitudes of the state' there are more deserving uses of an artist's time than to re-present the lurid and greedy colours of billboards and television commercials.

James Aulich may berate Roger Scruton as one of those Westerners who, like Peter Fuller and Andrew Brighton, embarked on an aesthetic crusade to Czechoslovakia in the late 80s, but Scruton's emphasis on 'spiritual absolutes, existential meaning and beauty' was perceptive in the sense that he understood before many others this changing role of art. Indeed, as the internationalist trend in the visual arts continues to pre-empt any political move towards true European union, it is perhaps time to re-examine the values of those seemingly reactionary individuals such as the composer Ralph Vaughan Williams, whose ideas preceded Scruton or Fuller's by some 50 years.

As far back as 1942 Vaughan Williams warned that when 'the United

States of Europe becomes a fact, each nation must have something to bring to the common stock of good'.[22] Opposed to a Europe populated by 'good Europeans' sharing a universal language in the arts, he asserted that 'what each nation offers must not be a bad imitation of what other nations do better': in terms of the banality of Knížák's comment on culture and tradition, Jeff Koons wins hands down.

Fuller himself was quick to warn against ignorance or xenophobia too but argued passionately for an 'informed provincialism which looks for immediate meaning in local forms, and finds its larger sense through affiliation to a national tradition'.[23] Whilst both were pleading a case for a British tradition, such statements are relevant for all nations. Knížák, on the other hand, rides high on the internationalism that bears little relevance to a true Czech tradition and instead exploits the rude truths of artists such as Keith Haring, whose merchandising sensibility took him to the Berlin Wall. Whilst Haring salvaged some street credibility out of his graffiti excursion, Knížák's own contribution to the decoration of the wall earned him an award.

Marcela Pánková perhaps sums up the crisis for Czech art when she says that 'the value of art cannot be measured by the degree to which it has been prohibited. The danger lies in something else. How will it handle the newly acquired burden of Freedom?'[24]

The answer, sadly, is that Czech art today, for the most part, is not handling the burden of a newly acquired freedom, it is selling out to the internationalism that in this country has already revealed itself as a hollow philosophy. Just what a state Czech art is in can be glimpsed in the work of Tansy Spinks, a young artist who graduated from The Royal College of Art in London in 1984 and visited Prague in 1990-91 with the aid of an Academic Research Award from the British Council.

Her *Prague Portrait Series* ironically is a body of work that looks more 'Czech' than work by Czechs! Maps, city squares crowded with people, even a letter written by Kafka, and the characteristic light of a Prague sky, parody art from Czechoslovakia at a time when its future was perhaps most uncertain.

Contemporaneously with Spinks' making of the *Prague Portraits* however, Květa Válova was painting her *They are Leaving*. The monolithic scale of the leaning figures in the painting recalls the departure of the last Soviet troops. It is a highly sensitive and humane portrayal of a dejected body of men whose entire purpose and own future was then being brought into question. It could be that if the Czech's awake from their international dream, it is Válova who could save them from an anaesthetising Western art value system.

While more cumbersome and self conscious than Henry Moore's war-time shelter drawings, the figures in *They are Leaving*, are nevertheless similar to the apolitical anonymity of human types revealed in Australian artist Peter Booth's landscapes. Valova may be among the few artists in the Czech and Slovak Republics who offer any hope for an authentic Czech art to emerge, for she opts not for a mannered stylisation and, furthermore, rejects the tacit assumption that the intellectual idea can carry art alone. What she does is marry the universal truths of art with a personal vision based upon her experiences at a particular historical point. Most of all, she does not rarefy a now redundant intelligentsia, and if it is there at all it is implicit in the work. Her painting does not parade its politics like some *samizdat* rag or Civic Forum poster, it is painting which functions first and foremost in terms of a painterly fine art tradition: of human scale and of imaginative endeavour.

It is a painting which may not fulfil the requirements put by Scruton – spiritual absolutes, existential meaning and beauty – but given that it is the product of an extreme cultural experience, like the work of Jaroslav Róna and Petr Nikl, it comes pretty close. In such work we glimpse, perhaps for the last time, a truly authentic national Czech art.

ABOVE: Tansy Spinks, two-layer photographic collage from Prague Portrait Series, *1992, 91.5x61cm; BELOW: Tansy Spinks, two-layer photographic collage from* Prague Portrait Series, *1992, 66x76x10cm*

Notes

1 T Pospiszyl, 'The Stunners and The Neo-Stunners', *Europe Without Walls: Art, Posters and Revolution 1989-93*, J Aulich and T Wilcox (eds), Manchester City Art Gallery, 1993.

2 'View from Route 65: Prague to Bratislava', *Artscribe*, May 1989.

3 'Czechoslovak Art Now', *Art Monthly* 157, June 1992.

4 My response to Juler's report appeared in *Art Monthly* l9, August 1992.

5 *Artline* 'Migrating West' V/5, 1991; Artworks 'Prague Spring in a British Winter', 1991; *The Antique Collector*, 'In Search of A Heritage', February 1992.

6 Preface to 'A New Spirit in Painting' exhibition catalogue, Royal Academy of Arts, 1981.

7 Catalogue essay to exhibition of work by Petr Nikl, Prague Town Hall Gallery, 1989.

8 J Aulich, 'Through the Looking Glass: Visual Expression in Central Europe 1989-93', *Europe Without Walls,* op cit.

9 The text cited carries the by-line 'Pavla Pecinková 1992'. The source of the photocopy in my possession is unknown, as is the title.

10 Aulich and Wilcox, *Europe without Walls*, op cit.

11 'Art, Nationalism and the Fin de Siècle', *A Golden Age: 1896-1914*, Corvina/Barbican Art Gallery, 1990.

12 Aulich and Wilcox, *Europe without Walls*, op cit.

13 Dojc's most recent exhibition in Britain was 'In and Out of Czechoslovakia' at the Zelda Cheatle Gallery.

14 'Elective Affinities', curated by Penelope Curtis.

15 M Pánková, 'Report From Bohemia', *Europe Without Walls,* op cit.

16 Like many art journalists, Vann travelled to Czechoslovakia on a British Council grant and published a series of articles during the early part of 1989.

17 J Aulich, 'Through the Looking Glass', op cit.

18 L Hudson, 'The Cult of the Fact', Jonathon Cape, 1972.

19 Germaine Greer, 'Mozic and the Revolution', *Oz*, October 1969, republished in *The Madwoman's Underclothes: Essays and Occasional Writings 1968-85*, Picador, 1986.

20 J Aulich, 'Through the Looking Glass', op cit.

21 J Aulich, 'Through the Looking Glass', op cit.

22 R Vaughan Williams, *National Music and Other Essays*, Oxford University Press, 1963.

23 *Art Monthly* 100, republished in *Seeing through Berger*, Claridge Press 1988.

24 M Pánková, op cit.

OPPOSITE: Milan Knížák: Czech Landscape No 1, 1990, 45x110x70cm; BELOW: Květa Válova, They are Leaving, *1990, oil on canvas, 150x320cm (diptych)*

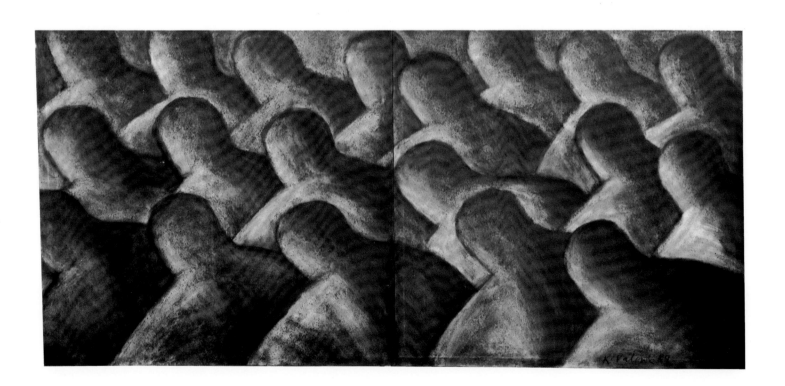

MILAN KNÍŽÁK
KILL YOURSELF AND FLY
An interview by Johan Pijnappel

Johan Pijnappel: You once mentioned you were probably born with a preference for disharmony. Is there a reason for this attitude in your work and life?

Milan Knížák: You know my father was a teacher who taught art and mathematics. A very funny combination. And maybe this combination has really defined my life, because I also have one foot in real pragmatic mathematical work and the other foot in dreams and craziness. I was always like that, I always felt very old, very mature, but on the other hand very crazy, young. For me, at the beginning of the 60s, an action was not a new page in the history of art but a very social act, a new way of life. Therefore I always say 'Art is a life-style', because for me art is not a separate work which I can exhibit. You know I can exhibit, that's no problem, but that's not the reason, not the final point. It is important for me that the artpiece itself is not the end result. The end result for me is the change which happens. It's a means of communication, it's a word, it's some kind of a psychic bridge between people. And even if you never experience that then it should be like that. I think about art as a means of communication and not as a treasure, something that is nice, beautiful and has value.

JP: The cultural and intellectual climate in Czechoslovakia was deeply changed between 1949 and 1953 by the politics of Gotwald: 'The umwertung der Werten' (the change of values). Then in 1960 when the CSSR was founded, everything was treated according to Marxist-Leninist values. How did you function as a student in the art academy with such a totalitarian way of communicating?

MK: You know, I was kicked out of all the schools, even the Academy of Visual Arts I'm the President of now. This is very funny, you know. When I was in the previous school, our class went to visit a very famous old artist who was professor and former President of the Academy. He had a very big and nice studio, but I was not allowed to visit him because they were afraid I would insult him . . . and his studio is now mine! I nearly died laughing when I came and I saw that this was the place where I was going to work.
Of course there were many problems during my student days and afterwards. I was taken by the police many, many times. I was in prison about three hundred times, maybe more or less but many hundreds of times.

JP: Was it possible in the beginning of the 60s in the CSSR to get information about contemporary Western art?

MK: There was one man in Prague whom I met in 1964, and that was my first contact with any information from outside. He was a very famous art-critic and his name was Jindrich Chalupecky. He was the only man in Czechoslovakia at that time who was interested in modern art, who had some art magazines and who was in contact with interesting modern artists from abroad. I was very happy that I could see their art and see that there were some people in the world who were similar to me; that was a big help because I felt very isolated here. You know everybody was just laughing at me. I remember there was a little cafe where I put on an exhibition because I didn't get a chance in an official gallery. An older artist and a very famous art critic came and they were killing themselves laughing. What I was doing was nothing, junk, a joke,

Milan Knížák

ABOVE: Small Environment on the Street, 1962-1964; BELOW: Game of War, 1965

something crazy and stupid, not art at all. Therefore when I found that there were some people around the world who thought a little bit like me I was extremely happy.

JP: When did you get more personal contact with European and American artists?

MK: Chalupecky sent photographs and descriptions of my work to some people. They liked it very much and they immediately started to make contact with me, people like Allan Kaprow, George Maciunas and Wolf Vostell. Allan Kaprow at that time was publishing the big book *Assemblage, Environments and Happening*. He put me in the best place, at the very end just before him. I was 25 years old and immediately became known world-wide as an artist. What I was doing here in Prague was very different from the others and it surprised Allan Kaprow very much so therefore he put it in the book. George Maciunas sent me many, many Fluxus pieces and Wolf Vostell published my pieces in *Décollage* magazine. This all happened after 1965 and I immediately got an invitation to go to the States, which I couldn't accept because I didn't have a passport.

JP: Was Fluxus an art movement you could identify with?

MK: Fluxus for me, I discovered later, was conservative according to my ideas, according to what I was thinking at that time. The whole Fluxus movement – I mean Fluxus not Happenings – was conservative, because they stayed on the stage. They made art, they made art pieces like concerts. And I wanted to get out of the galleries. I wanted to dissolve in the crowd. I wanted to keep art anonymous. I didn't want people to know I was making art. I wanted just to dig some kind of ditch in front of the house so that people couldn't get out. I wanted to bring my ideas into the stream of life. And Fluxus in that way was very conservative for me.

JP: Where were your actions from 1963-68 done, for example *A Walk into the New World*?

MK: 'New World' is how you would translate the name of the street I was living in at that time. This was very symbolic. It's still there. It's a very old, small street behind Prague Castle. Long ago very poor people lived there, and it was like a village in the middle of Prague. It was very nice with small houses and very narrow streets surrounded by big castles and churches. But there in the little valley it was almost forgotten. It was for me beautiful to be there. Even though the place I was staying in was not mine and was completely bad and unhealthy, I loved it, and the name was gorgeous, it just matched my ideas. But I made actions in many other significant places like the famous Charles Bridge. I was working at that time, in the middle of the 60s, as a janitor of those bridge towers. It wasn't much work and I had the keys so I could go there any time, even at night. There I made the action *The Other Object*. Another one was done at the observation tower in Prague, which looks like a small Eiffel tower. Over there I tried to do an action *Fold Two Metres Big Paper Glider*, but they kicked me out immediately.

JP: One of the groups you then founded to express your ideas was 'Group Aktuel'. Can you describe their intentions?

MK: We wanted to talk directly to people. We didn't want to create complicated media, complicated galleries. We wanted to influence people directly with anything which is strong and direct. You know, at that time we had the idea that art is something which can change a lot. Maybe it is not true but when you are young and enthusiastic then you think that with art you can change the world. Maybe you can, but maybe not as directly as we thought at that time. But we were convinced that it was possible and therefore we wanted to influence people directly.

JP: In the middle of the 60s, more people showed openly they were against the policy of President Antonin Novodny. There was more freedom at that time. How did you experience this?

MK: Well that didn't count for me. Novodny's men saw me at the castle, with a girl who was working there and who always helped to make pictures. At that time I had very long hair. Instantly he gave an order to the police to catch all the long-haired people and cut their hair. They did it because of me. It was very, very funny.

JP: When was it possible for you to travel abroad for the first time?

MK: In 1968, during the Prague Spring, they gave me a passport. But while I was waiting for an American visa, the Russians came. Then 40 days later I left for the States because I got a visa. I did not have the time to wait for the proper time. It was only possible in 1968. Before I had no passport. As I wanted to stay a little longer in the USA they prolonged my exit visa three times. In 1970 I wanted to go to Japan but they would not prolong it any more. They said I had to go home. If not you become a refugee. I didn't want to escape so I said all right, I'll come home. I was naive. I thought if I came home freely maybe they'd let me go out again. Of course not. The day I got home they took my passport and gave me so many problems.

JP: How was the freedom of the democratic USA compared to Prague in 1968?

MK: The Prague Spring in 1968 was so free, so wonderful that New York compared to Prague at that time was a jail. New York is OK, but Prague was much softer, much more human. Only in 1968 of course. I didn't feel the freedom in New York as something special, it was for me worse than in Prague because the Americans are like sheep, you know. They don't talk to the police, they are afraid.

JP: In the 1970s the freedom of 68 completely disappeared. Under the command of Bruzek and Miroslav Válek, the Ministers of Culture of the Czech Republic and Slovakia, the cultural scene became a cemetery. What were your experiences with the government at that time?

MK: The only representatives of the government who talked to me were policemen. They wanted to punish me and it was very, very complicated. I had only problems with the President. I was sent to prison for two years for a book of my art that I made. There were two charges. One for the book and the second for my documents which I gave to Hanns Sohm. He was in Prague and was later caught at the border of Germany, and kept in prison for two days. Because he was an old man and had been in the war, he went completely out of his mind.

   When I was sent to prison for two years many people protested. In many places such as the Stedelijk Museum in Holland, there were petitions printed for people to sign in protest. Many thousands of signatures were sent to the President. And the President talked about me on television. He said that I was a very bad man. That was a very funny situation. I came to visit my family, my father and mother and my mother invited me to have some dinner. While we sat around the table, the TV was on, and the President was talking. Suddenly he started to talk about me in a very bad way. It was very unpleasant. I sent him a telegram immediately saying that he had to apologise and that all he said was a lie. When I sent it to him the people in the post office said I was out of my mind. But I did it, I was not afraid. I started to fight and it saved me a little bit. But they gave me one extra charge. He said I was making pornographic paintings and selling them to Germany. As you know I was making no paintings at all at that time. It was so stupid.

JP: There were many people at that time who fled to the countryside to be able to

ABOVE: Sjaman Cloths, *1965-1970; BELOW:* Game of War, *1965*

give expression to their own ideas. In the cities pop groups like Plastic People and The Universe sang about another way of living. You were making actions like *Actionen die nicht geschehen können* (Actions that cannot happen). How were you working at that time?

MK: Plastic People for me was not that progressive. Aktuel, which I created was also a group. We had a concert together with Plastic People. Chalupecky when he heard it – he was an old man not experienced in rock and roll – said that compared to Aktuel, Plastic People was a band which should play in a cafe. Later on Plastic People had many troubles because they were mixed up with politics. When journalists wanted to publish bad reviews about them in newspapers and magazines they always used my songs. The texts Plastic People had were just not strong enough so they always used my songs as examples. I used to write to the magazines saying that they should correct the reviews and say they were my songs. That was very funny. There were songs like 'I Love You and Lenin', 'Sons of Bolshevism', 'Rats go off to War', 'The Bolshevik Messiah'. All these texts were against the regime. I was always laughing at the group Plastic People, because they just made very simple music with political influence. That is not enough. For me it was much more important to make music which brings new ideas, not only because it is mixed with politics. My politics was to make my work as good as possible, as deep, as strong as possible. The government did not like it at all. Plastic People didn't get busted for their work but they sometimes got busted for provocation. Like if somebody says you are a stupid Bolshevik or whatever. For me that's not a reason to be busted. When I was in jail it was always because of my work.

JP: Besides actions and music you were also making architectural proposals in outer space. Was this for you also a vision of the new world?

MK: Architecture came a little later but started in the middle of the 60s. *City in the Desert* was a real vision. It was a complex plan. Not only for the buildings, for the environment, for the fashion but also for the political system. It was a complete vision of a new city. Later I wrote books about immaterial architecture; *Architectural Thoughts, A Trial of Non-systematic Introduction into the Problematic of Immaterial Architecture* and a book about architecture like music, architecture which happens in the space in your own mind. I made many plans to use architecture which is constructed from different materials and provokes your own way of life and living.

JP: You were driven to these projects because you were living in an oppressed society?

MK: I could not publish and could not exhibit. And I loved so much to work. I was always dreaming about my life. I was creating works for my self because I couldn't do it in reality. When I showed my designs of furniture and fashion to professional designers they could not believe that I produced thousands of ideas without realisation. They could not believe it because they had one simple idea and a hundred realisations. And I had so many ideas and I said I don't care. I just did it because I lived in my own space and it didn't hurt me to make things which weren't realised; in that space it was much nicer to be dressed in dreams, to live in a dream house. On the other hand my pieces, my furniture, my architecture are very useful. They may have a little bit of something which brings a new way of using them. For instance Michael Berger in Wiesbaden has a writing desk I made for him, and says he is very happy with it.

JP: At the end of the 70s the DAAD in Berlin invited you . . .

MK: I was invited before. I got the first invitation I guess at the end of 1974. But I couldn't go then because I hadn't a passport, they didn't let me go.

JP: Then why did the government give you a passport in 1979?

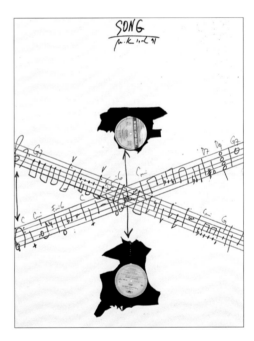

OPPOSITE ABOVE: Hat for a Crowd, 1973; BELOW: Creatures from New Paradise, 1990; ABOVE: Milan Knížák with his Dwarf Collection on the Charles Bridge, Prague, 1989; BELOW: Song, 1991

MK: It was very complicated. A famous Czech artist who lived in Paris also got the same grant from DAAD and they let him go in 1979. I made a protest to the government: 'Why he can go and why not me?' We started to fight, they said he is old and I said that has nothing to do with it. Then the minister gave me and my wife, Marianne, a travel permit, one way there and one way back for the whole year. They thought we would never come back. They were very surprised we came back. But it was very hard. Marianne had two kids and they had to stay here. It was not nice. And because she doesn't travel by aeroplane she stayed the whole year in Berlin. She could not leave East Berlin because it is in East Germany.

For all those years Marianne and I were having to fight every day. Our nerves were almost broken. Like for instance our son had to go to school to welcome Brezhnev. At four o'clock in the morning before that meeting the police came and took me into jail.

JP: At that time you made the work *Kill Yourself and Fly*. Were times so hard?

MK: It was a song I wrote that had this title. For me it meant not only to protest but also to get rid of your old personality. Trying to get rid all the stupid things you have to live through. Getting rid of your weaknesses. Flying for me means something very symbolic, like being above yourself, being above your everyday problems. 'Kill and fly' means getting free. But at that time I wrote it as Kill yourself and fly, Kill yourself and sing. Singing also is a free activity which express freedom, luck and happiness.

JP: In the 80s in Czechoslovakia there was a 'parallel culture' beside the officially controlled culture of the totalitarian state. Were you involved with the parallel culture?

MK: At the very beginning, because I did these art events which made me very famous, they wanted me to become the leader of that underground movement. They call that the underground. But I did not agree because many of those people were too primitive. And I said I don't want to be the one-eyed leader, leading the blind. I don't want to manipulate the crowd. I want to be independent. So I stayed independent. I was not for the government, I was not with the so-called decents, with the opposition. They were for me also very narrow minded.

JP: You are very much interested in Eastern philosophy. How did you encounter this, and was it Buddhism or Hinduism?

MK: More Hinduism I would say. I met a yogi and started to do yoga twice in my life. Once at the beginning of the 70s. And once in the middle of the 70s, which was for me very important. It lasted for five years. I was pure vegetarian of course, no fish, no tea, no coffee, no alcohol, no eggs, no nothing. I was hardly exercising and I got pretty high. When we came back from Berlin I was very sick. Then I had a choice: to stay with yoga, or to leave society, because it was impossible for me to live both lives together. I could not go by a streetcar, it was all stinking. I had nothing against people but I just couldn't live with them. Then I was thought, 'Do I have such a right to leave human society?' Then I decided I still had a duty to stay because I can still do something with my work. Then I went to the first bar I could see and had beer and sausages which was horrible. Since then I have had many physical problems, but it was the only possible thing for me to do. I came directly back to life. But the state of mind is still inside me, it helped me a lot. It was a very good experience. But you know in this world, in the East of Europe, in this country which was under big pressure, I didn't dare to leave our society completely. It's too selfish. Maybe that is mistaken but I had such a feeling at that time.

JP: At the end of the 80s Gorbachev came and there was more open resistance in Czechoslovakia. What was your experience with the new art groups at that time like 'The Harde Hovede' and '12/15'?

ABOVE: Angel in front of the Castle in Prague, *1990; BELOW:* Fathers of the Homeland No 2, *1990*

MK: These people were very young, very strong and aggressive. They had many friends, many other young people. I think what they made at that time was not real art but more like education. They brought many influences, many post-modern styles from outside and showed them to the public. But the circumstances didn't changed much. The last exhibition cancelled in Czechoslovakia was mine. I was supposed to have an exhibition in November 1989. This exhibition was forbidden in September 1989, because you have to plan the exhibition and it was cancelled.

Prague never dared to put on an exhibition of my work, but Brno put on my biggest exhibition in 1989. They published the catalogue *Milan Knížák 1953-1988*. Just that it was possible for them to publish it was so great. It was unbelievable. They were afraid about it in Brno. Thousands of people came, it was great.

Up until now the National Gallery has never bought an artwork by me. One print came into their collection by accident when they bought a big art collection in Germany of many artists.

JP: In 1989 there was a glorious (so-called velvet) revolution in Czechoslovakia. Some people wanted you to become the Minister of Culture. Was Havel in favour of this plan?

MK: I'm not enthusiastic about Havel. I think he's not intellectual enough. For me he is bound by middle-class art, he is a middle-class writer. He writes very simple, conventional plays. His cultural programme at the present is very low. Many people wanted me to but even now I wouldn't take it, because I don't want to be mixed up with politics. I don't want to join those parties. I want to stay on my own. Then I am free, I can say what I want. I'm in the media very often and it means I can influence a lot. I can sit on many boards of trustees. I have a lot of possibilities to influence culture in Czechoslovakia. But being the minister, being an office worker who is responsible to a party . . .

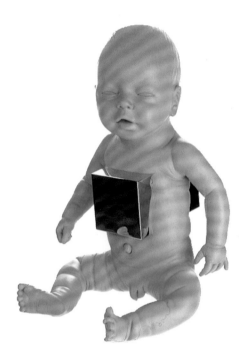

JP: Among your latest work there a work with the title *New Paradise*. Elements of it look like types of aeroplanes and strange animals with fishes' tails but different fronts. Is it again an imaginary paradise for you like in your earlier work?

MK: Many ideas from the past come again to me with a new force. I have a vision of a new existence, because now at the end of the millennium, and after so many catastrophes of ecology, we are in a very bad period and we have to handle it very carefully. How to go forward? In a way young, small countries playing at nationalism are very dangerous. With this piece I would like to tell people that we have to respect any kind of creature. Therefore I made strange animals and other creatures which look like aeroplanes, because I want people not to tell lies. Any kind of a creature has the same value as us. We are not privileged animals here in our world, the globe. We are one of many. And therefore I made this and I'm working further on pieces like that.

Also I made a piece of 12 masks, with six knives and called that *First Twelve*, like 12 apostles, 12 new, strange people who may bring a new religion. In my vision now it is not like a vision of people living in a city, having special clothes, special houses, special systems. It is more warning people, telling them to come back to themselves and try to live more peacefully, and be more friendly to anything which is here in this world. I'm trying to get rid of that anthropocentric way of thinking which is for me very dangerous. I say always that stone, for instance, lives like us. Only its breath lasts maybe five million years. You know therefore we can't live together, because our breath takes two seconds and its breath is maybe five million years. It means therefore we don't meet. But it does not mean we are different creatures. We are creatures of the same system, of the same world. Just the time scale is different.

Prague, 9 October 1993

ABOVE: Biblical Landscape, *1990, lasergraph;*
BELOW: Baby Mutant, *1992*

A COMMUNAL CONNECTION

ILYA KABAKOV AND CONTEMPORARY RUSSIAN ART
Peter Suchin

'Illustration as a way to Survive' is the title of a current, internationally seen exhibition of the work of two contemporary Russian artists, Ilya Kabakov and Ülo Sooster.[1] As a show juxtaposing the work of, on the one hand, an artist of international repute and near-mythic status (Kabakov) and, on the other, one who is virtually unknown in the West (Sooster), the two-pronged thrust of the exhibition offers an interesting analogy or contrast. It is less than a decade since the former Union of Soviet Socialist Republics allowed out into the West such major artists as Kabakov who, even in their own country, kept their personal, distinct, unofficial work hidden and in some cases unrealised until the Western art market allowed for its practical presentation through the patronage of major galleries and collectors. The other side of the situation of the Russian contemporary artist is obscurity and the carrying out of a practice that takes as its norm an only difficult and unacceptable pathway with regard to its display.

'Illustration as a way to Survive' is an exhibition actually designed by Kabakov himself, and the presentation of his own work alongside that of his (now deceased) friend Ülo Sooster serves to heighten another aspect of the life, at least prior to perestroika, of the Russian artist. The sharp contrast to be drawn by the display is that of a way of working. For Kabakov and Sooster's generation (they were born in 1933 and 1924 respectively) the characteristic mode of making a living as an artist was to work as a state artist, accepting without question the official aesthetic/political line of Socialist Realism. It was a question of serving an ideological end with one's work, providing a model, within one's pictures, of an idealised and idealising way of life. As an alternative to this central channel for artistic practice, the job of acting as an illustrator of children's books seemed to offer a viable alternative modus operandi for those trained in the Russian art schools.

The contrast afforded by the exhibition to which I refer gives an airing, however, to something more than the simple paradigm of official versus unofficial illustrative or aesthetic practice. Examining both the show itself and its accompanying catalogue, one discovers that two ways of dealing with the burden of officialdom in the realm of the visual arts are presented here. Sooster took a path which was, it appears, bound to lead to a series of difficulties with the censor. In his work as an illustrator of children's books he attempted to conflate his own particular aesthetic concerns (we will call these Surrealism) with those of the work he was commissioned to do. His personal obsessions and philosophico-aesthetic speculations, those aspects of himself which other artists might confine to the privacy of their studios, were openly integrated into the drawings and paintings made to illustrate mass-produced books. The result was many clashes with the censor, with publishers and their editors, and therefore much difficulty in selling work and with making a living from that work. This refusal to compromise may be read as heroic; in any case Sooster's work, though often finally published after numerous editorial alterations, provoked for this artist as many difficulties as it in other respects resolved.

In acute and intriguing contrast, the illustration work of Ilya Kabakov raised for itself and its author very few awkwardnesses or moments of conflict. The reason for this is clearly explained during an interview between Kabakov and Joseph Bakstein. Kabakov remarks:

Since what motivated me when I received orders for illustrations was not a desire to create unique works of art for books and not a love for children but the goal was only to earn money, furthermore as quickly as possible so that I still had some time left for something else, then for me there was no choice here – to insist upon my artistic 'quest' or to master

'The Man Who Flew into Space From His Apartment', from Ten Characters, 1981-88, *detail, photo D James Dee*

**ILLUSTRATION
AS A WAY TO SURVIVE:**

ILYA KABAKOV AND ÜLO SOOSTER

ABOVE: Kabakov and Sooster, Illustration as a way to Survive, *exhibition designed by Kabakov and installed in the Centre for Contemporary Arts, Glasgow, July to September 1993; BELOW:* Illustration as a way to Survive, *brochure for the Glasgow presentation of the exhibition showing a book illustration by Ülo Sooster*

the existing 'style', this 'norm' in as short a time as possible. Such a hermaphrodite had to be born – a combination of artist and editor who draws that which he knew would be, and could not not be, accepted.[2]

Kabakov's approach as an illustrator was then to conform unreservedly to the official modes of expression and subject matter, not to relentlessly introduce into his illustrations personal, privately important philosophies such as those foregrounded by Sooster at all levels of his practice but to make, rather, a sharp distinction between his personal work and that work required by the Moscow publishing houses, ultimately, that is, by the state. It is this very carefully planned division between a public and a private face that characterised Kabakov's practice prior to his recent but very far-reaching fame in the West.

Perhaps a few remarks outlining the general context of very recent concerns in Russian art and aesthetics are in order before focusing in more detail on Kabakov's undeniably distinct work.

Just as Kabakov is becoming recognised in the West as one of the very major figures in Russian art over the last two or three decades, a new, 'third wave' of younger artists is beginning to make its presence felt. One of the most notable events affecting the Moscow art fraternity in recent years took place on 15 April 1990 in Moscow itself, when the painter Favid Bogdalov took to effacing a number of exact reproductions of works by key individuals in Moscow's (that is Russia's) alternative art scene. This performance of excision or obliteration took the form of Bogdalov covering the reproductions with white paint, at one and the same moment signifying a recognition of the 'alternative' scene as much as suggesting that that 'tradition' of dissenting Moscow artists (Eric Bulatov and Kabakov were amongst those selected) was to be relegated to the past. The so-called 'White Event' may in fact be read in various ways but it is clear that a prominent intention is the degrading of an alternative grouping of artists that had, in the eyes of some, become much too official an oppositional force.[3]

The work of the younger generation that claims to replace or aspires to overthrow the previous generation (the 'Sots-Art', that is the pseudo-conceptual grouping that includes such important

figures as Kabakov) apparently tends towards a kind of seeking-out of a clean slate, the finding of a zone of values that are intended to be ideology-free, new and untainted, formed against a background of an art that had been, whether in its official or unofficial form, loaded with unashamedly political values. Socialist Realism, as the official doctrine amongst artists and art lovers alike, stood back-to-back with the covertly engaged 'independent' clutch of artists critical of the state and of the dogmatic aesthetics it chose to promote. Among this new wave of artists, for the most part born in the 1960s, are figures such as Gor Chakal (employing images taken from the 'romantic' moments of Russian cinema), Andrej Besukladnikov (whose *The Unknown Woman* operates by juxtaposing, in the manner of, say, Victor Burgin, two photographs, one of a pretty young woman staring at the viewer, the other of a subway car), and three artists who operate under the name 'Medical Hermeneutics' (Sergei Anufriev, Yurii Leiderman and Pavel Peppershtein).[4] These young artists all display a concern for a deliberate forgetting of the politically loaded unofficial art practices that on the whole preceded their own. Their concern is for an 'art for art's sake' range of approaches (a situation that, according to the critic Viktor Misiano is an entirely new one for Russian artists). Already beginning to be known in the West, these and other recently emerging artists do not have, it seems to me, either the complexity or the aesthetic weight of someone like Kabakov, whose track record as a convincingly serious, one might say major, artist is already fixing itself in the West.

For the remainder of this account I will concentrate on Kabakov's work. This is not to dismiss the more recent trends emerging in Russian art, but it is Kabakov who remains prominent as the key figure of recent years. Notwithstanding the many complicated shifts in the relationship between Russia and the West over the past ten or 15 years a full, unclouded picture of Russian art practice has yet to emerge. That picture is already complex and bound to increase in its complexity as more and more Russian artists gain access to Western galleries and Western media. The information on Kabakov is already considerable, the exhibitions and publications already many and varied. I will restrict myself to but a few examples from his prodigious output.

Kabakov was born in Djnepropetrovsk in the Ukraine. Moving to Moscow in 1939 he eventually graduated from that city's Surikov Art Institute and from 1955 onwards worked as a children's book illustrator for the Detgiz Publishing House. It was largely through the activities of a New York dealer, Ronald Feldman, who had established contacts with Russia's underground artists in 1976, that Kabakov became known in the West. It wasn't until 1988 that Feldman managed to stage a show of Kabakov's work outside Russia (this was *Ten Characters*, shown in New York in April of that year).

Ten Characters is undoubtedly a central work in Kabakov's oeuvre. It is a multi-media piece designed to make manifest, through a series of linked installations, the highly idiosyncratic behaviour and environment of ten characters who live out their lives as part of the population of Moscow's many communal apartments. Reading the artist's descriptions of the characters in the catalogue that accompanies the piece, it's easy almost to forget the actual existence of the constructed rooms themselves. Kabakov's stories call up lucid pictures of convincingly distinct personages. As he writes at the beginning of the catalogue:

> When I submerge into my childhood world, I see it inhabited by a number of the most strange and comic individuals, neighbours of our large communal apartment. Each one of them, it seemed to me then, had an unusual idea, one all-absorbing passion belonging to him alone.

As within the Western field of postmodernist cultural production there's an ambiguity of authorship in Kabakov's work that is not a little difficult to clarify. The ten characters are plausibly constructed on paper. They are at one and the same moment believable and yet far too eccentric – at least some of them – to be fully believed in as actual once or still existing people, real people trapped (yet not inescapably imprisoned) in the world of the cramped, dull and dilapidated communal culture of the Moscow apartment. It's as though Kabakov really did once encounter these eccentric and obsessive collectors, artists and musicians and has chosen to record their passions as a way of proving that people were not entirely swamped by the oppressive babblings of the pre-perestroika Russian state.

Yet figures who build mini rocket propulsion systems to blast themselves out through the roof into hypothetical energy channels, or who save drowning men without even leaving the space of their room, can't really be accepted as characters who exist in actuality. Their excessivity is more likely a deliberate exaggeration, a deliberate taking-to-extremes of a type of activity that may well be the sanity-saving vehicle Kabakov appears to suggest it is. These serious amateurs are described as though each spends all his free time engaged in the pursuit of a single, intensely personal task, a task that not only consumes their energy and interest like a glorified hobby but actually structures their very existence. The very self of each subject who is discussed in Kabakov's stories is defined by the peculiarities at play in the presentations. The implausibility of the lengths to which the ten characters go in following their obsessions is in fact what makes these people plausible, not anonymous inhabitants of miserable apartments, unknown workers for the socialist state but, on the contrary, absolutely distinct individuals, living out authentic lives, authentic selves each in the personal space offered, if feebly and awkwardly, by their private rooms. The focus in the stories and in their connected constructions is upon the visual, verbal and physical manifestation of an acute individuality, a marking out of the personal within the boundaries of an environment that must needs be communal, indistinct, aggressively unpleasant in its absence of privacy, of 'personal space'.

Kabakov has commented on the inescapability in Soviet life of the ceaseless babble, not just of the state but of the orthodoxies and naturalised beliefs of one's neighbours in the communal apartment. One is surrounded for most of one's life with the language of cliche, drumming into one's psyche a lexicon of state-serving concepts and constraints. The subject is worn down by such a discourse and to replace it one seeks out silences, gaps, breaks in the relentless gush of mediocre words:

> Amid the domination of an ocean of words, a high level of reaction of the body of society to the omnipresence of text is inescapable. And lacunae of silence arise – there is a

ABOVE: 'The Man Who Flew into Space From His Apartment', from Ten Characters, *1981-88 detail; BELOW: 'The Man Who Never Threw Anything Away', from* Ten Characters, *1981-88, detail*

need for these chinks and apertures, a gravitation towards speechlessness. In the general repressive sea of words, speechlessness is perceived as a revelation. Silence and non-speech are identified with a magical existence . . . Communal articulated speech is ponderous, malicious, negative. Efforts to go beyond the speech of the everyday . . . are a bewitching opportunity not to speak but to fashion something inspired by the sweet visions, magical sights, and original worlds that have, as it were, unfolded before one's eyes.[7]

Ten Characters could be said to be in one sense on the side of silence and in favour of the visual, 'in praise' of the object as extant, clearly present thing. It is a piece of work very much concerned with the physical, with making, constructing, collecting. There's also something of the 'magical sights, and original worlds' of which Kabakov speaks. Language is itself omnipresent in Kabakov's assemblages but he redresses the balance, destroys the destruction enacted by the prattle of everyday speech (which, as in the West, is a loaded language, an ideological tool). In his deep concern with language, for the telling of pointed and ground-regaining stories as much as for his endless inspection of the linguistic sign as bearer of determined opinion Kabakov has affinities with conceptual art and its offspring, as well as with the analyses of linguistic norms carried out by Barthes, Lacan and others in our own culture. One thinks also of the likes of Schwitters and Duchamp, the latter being one in whom Kabakov has shown a keen interest.

Who are the 'ten characters' of the title? The title-descriptions act as a clue to the peculiar make-up of each of the personalities scrutinised and represented by Kabakov: 'The Man Who Flew into His Picture', 'The Man Who Collects the Opinions of Others', 'The Man Who Flew into Space From His Apartment', 'The Untalented Artist', 'The Short Man', 'The Composer Who Combined Music With Things and Images', 'The Collector', 'The Person Who Describes His Life Through Characters', 'The Man Who Saves Nikolai Viktorovich', and 'The Man Who Never Threw Anything Away'.

In the actual installation that comprises the work each figure is represented by a finely-constructed actual-size model of the occupant's room. The artist has assembled these spaces from a huge range of actual objects and materials – soil, string, wood, paper, cardboard, canvas, postcards and photographs, metal and plastic are some of the main materials employed (often in the form of found objects carefully arranged by Kabakov to form the singular cells of the communal building). I propose to give some detailed consideration to just one of the ten characters before concluding with a brief reference to other aspects of Kabakov's aesthetic production.

'The Man who Collects the Opinions of Others' relates the activities and theories of a philologist who believes that all opinions are arranged in circles. The *Ten Characters* catalogue text begins by setting the scene:

You could almost always catch him engaged in a rather strange occupation: he would throw some object on the floor in the corridor near his door – it could be an old boot, a dirty can of corned beef, a bunch of useless keys, or even a coat or old trousers. He would stand in his room, on the other side of the slightly opened door, with a notebook and pencil in his hands and he would wait to see what would happen in the corridor. If it were possible to see him from the side, then he usually reminded me of a fisherman, tense and alert, waiting with his rod in hand.

Someone's footsteps could be heard coming down the hallway. (It's a neighbour or someone he doesn't know going towards the kitchen or bathroom.) Having seen or banged into the strange object under their feet, each person says something appropriate to the occasion. And he, standing behind the door, immediately writes down in his notebook everything which is said, no matter what: a profound and long utterance, an exclamation of surprise, or some filthy curses which are common here . . .[8]

The narrator of this account, ostensibly Kabakov himself, gives further details of the philologist's theoretical speculations about the structure of opinions. We learn that there are three stages of opinion, arranged hierarchically. The first of these is the spontaneous utterance, the remark released in a moment of surprise, annoyance or stupefaction. This fast-formed opinion is like the moment when a stone thrown

'The Man Who Collects the Opinions of Others', from Ten Characters, *1981-88, detail, photo D James Dee*

49

into a lake hits the surface of the (previously calm) water.

The second stage of opinion is when the opinion in question is not a spontaneous utterance but rather one which is the result of careful consideration, is cautiously thought out, weighed, elaborate and finely formed: this is the 'mature' moment of opinion. It's a category of opinion that's precise, and the narrator is careful to point out that there are a multitude of opinions fixed at this point of development, in fact here there are as many opinions as there are different people. To pursue the analogy of the stones and the lake, we are here dealing with 'those even and clear circles, those fine and high waves which move along the surface of the water into which the stone drops.'[9]

The third stage of opinion is their moment of dissolution. It is the phase at which a given opinion collides with other viewpoints, other opinions and at which, as a result of this collision, it begins to break up, and finally it vanishes 'from the surface of being'.[10] Collectively the components of this little life-cycle of the opinion can be conceptualised visually as a series of conflicting, colliding ripples on the surface of a lake, as though 20 or so stones had been thrown in willy-nilly, at the same time. The ripples from the stones are of varying intensities and they travel across the lake in different directions, outwards of course, from the point at which each stone cuts through the surface of the water, hitting at diverse moments ripples generated by other stones, so that the top of the water forms a structure of intersecting tremors, a constellation, so to speak, of shaky, overlapping circles, each influencing and being influenced by the other circles with which they collide. This pattern of interpenetrating traces of the thrown stones represents a kind of map or chart of opinions, of how 'opinion' as a means of conceptualisation operates. As the ripples gradually die away new ripples, new opinions materialise and in their turn affect other, simultaneously extant points of view, until this 'new wave' of opinions gives way to another massive cluster of utterances.

As the narrator outlines the philologist's linguistic paradigm he presents us with yet one more example of how the philologist conspires to construct situations so that they work to produce more opinions for his collection:

After a short hesitation, and as though looking at me in doubt, near the end of our conversation he invited me into his room. It was almost empty . . . It was as though the room was waiting for something, as though something was supposed to happen in it . . . From a fairly large sack which was lying in the corner, he began to take out rather strange, and in general, old and sloppy things – an empty egg carton, a used broom, a plastic package filled with papers, a bunch of keys, a black rag – and he began to hang all of this along his bare walls . . .[11]

The narrator describes how, following the placing of each individual object on a nail on the wall the philologist produced a collection of pieces of paper, each bearing a short, meticulously inscribed phrase. These individual phrases were then attached to the wall in such a way that a number of them surrounded each of the things hanging there, so that the little pieces of text collectively formed a quite distinct, not unpretty 'wreath' around the various apparently discarded objects. These wreaths were really a visual rendering, a literal illustration of the circle of opinions triggered by the individual items taken from the sack. The philologist's theory of opinions thus took on a direct material-visual form. It was just when the narrator had recognised how elegantly, with what clear logic and indisputable beauty the philologist's ideas could be and actually had been presented that another development in the teasing out and taking down of opinions took place:

I looked around the room, and becoming more and more engrossed in its strange atmosphere, I began heatedly to try and persuade him to publish his discovery and maybe to show his exposition somewhere, at least in the form of a lecture. Possibly, this was a very important scientific discovery and proved some sort of special connection between the intellectual and visual spheres. Enthusiastically developing this idea, moving from one exhibit to another, I temporarily lost sight of my neighbour. But then I suddenly noticed that he hadn't interrupted my long speech even for a minute, and hadn't responded to my words with a single sound. I shut up and looked around . . . He was standing near the table, and with notebook in hand, he was carefully and

ABOVE: 'The Untalented Artist', from Ten Characters, *1981-88; OPPOSITE: 'The Man Who Never Threw Anything Away', from* Ten Characters, *1981-88, detail, photo D James Dee*

51

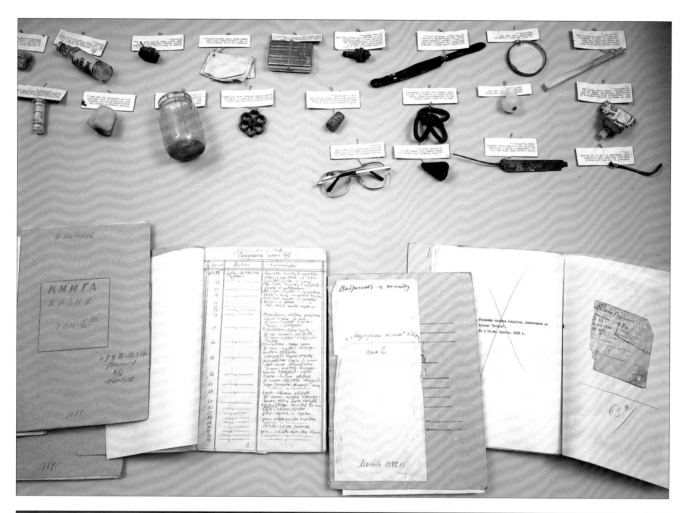

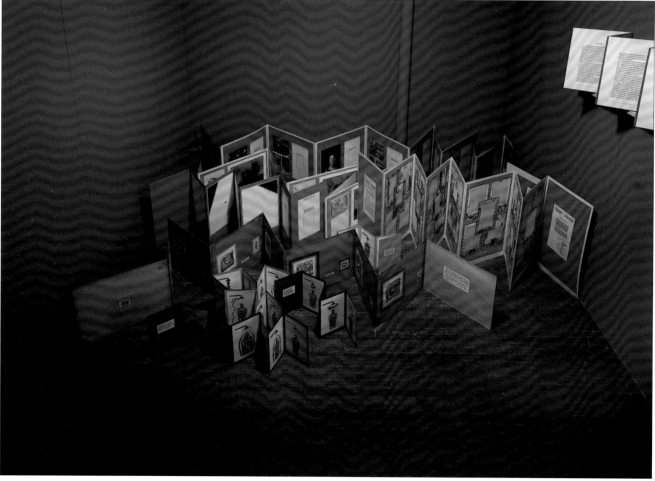

concentratedly writing down all that I had said in the heat of the moment.[12]

So the narrator, himself acting by the telling of his tale of 'The Man Who Collects the Opinions of Others' to record an opinion, a theory, a world-view offered by a philologist of a distinctly eccentric bent, finds that he himself has become a part of the philologist's re-search. There's something Kafkaesque about this blunt circularity as well as with regard to the near-relentless production of the structure formed by the hunting down of a new opinion. A meta-linguistic moment is reached, a point at which the mere collecting of spontaneous utter-ances linked to 'indiscriminate' objects becomes the cataloguing of an opinion about the cataloguing of opinions itself.

The circularity of this tale, its clever reflexivity, is typical of the accounts given of the other apartment internees and of the astuteness of Kabakov's work generally. One thinks of the incredible scenarios found in the novels of Raymond Roussel or, in another vein, of the pointed narratives of Dostoevsky or Chekhov, witty and worldly-wise and with the 'philosophical' features of the work buried within the form of the prose itself. So with Kabakov, whose intellectual interests perfectly interpenetrate the formal features of the assembled pieces. Though we never see any of the ten characters in person, their 'reality' is imprinted upon the objects of their pensive aesthetic attention. The neatly-annotated archive belonging to 'The Man Who Never Threw Anything Away'; the bright, brash posters, diagrams and trajectory plans left behind by 'The Man Who Flew into Space From His Apart-ment'; the minuscule labyrinth of images and texts laboriously pieced together by 'The Short Man': Collectively these 'portable museums' of melancholy memory objects reveal a glut of allu-sions, secret aspirations and lost, silent, subtle, slices of time.

For many years when Kabakov, in Soviet Russia, couldn't realise his large-scale projects, he produced albums of folded, painted, collaged cardboard. These small 'conceptual' works continue to be part of his output despite the grand scale made possible by his success in the West.[13] Just as *Ten Characters* gives us the 'ordinary' (yet enviably exceptional) man as hero these albums turn the ostensibly trivial into, through the power of word-play, some-thing that both disorientates and realigns the everyday. It is again Kabakov's close inspection of language that is in opera-tion here. There is something of the Russian modernist 'tradition' of radical reformulation and analysis of language (Khlebnikov, Kruchenykh, Shlovsky, Bakhtin) in Kabakov's multi-layered, multi-media work. It is this unremitting interest in the importance of the mun-dane, together with an overwhelming ability to 'make it strange', to transform and renew the received cultural, that is perceptual and linguistic, landscape in a manner pertinent to both the contempo-rary East and West that makes Kabakov's practice one of considerable critical significance amongst those in operation today.

Notes

1 The exhibition's tour itinerary (1992-94) is Kortrijk (Belgium), Birmingham (England), Glasgow (Scotland), Ramat Gan (Israel) and Vancouver (Canada). I would like to thank the staff of the Centre for Contem-porary Arts, Glasgow, for their assistance in the preparation of this essay.

2 *Ilustration as a Way to Survive*, catalogue p28.

3 On the implications of the 'White Event' see Viktor Misiano, 'Old-Fashioned Passion', *Flash Art* 158, May/June 1991, pp110-13.

4 See Anthony Iannacci, 'Psychedelia, Coke and Sherlock Holmes' (an interview with Medical Hermeneutics), *Artscribe* 83, September/October 1990, pp56-58.

5 Misiano, 'Old-Fashioned Passion', p111.

6 Ilya Kabakov, *Ten Characters*, ICA, London, 1989, p1.

7 Kabakov quoted in Victor Tupitsyn, 'From the Communal Kitchen', *Arts Magazine* 66, October 1991, p53.

8 Kabakov, *Ten Characters*, p9.

9 Ibid, p10.

10 Ibid, p10.

11 Ibid, pp10-11.

12 Ibid, p11.

13 These small, easily portable albums are like fragments of the larger installations though they are designed as works in their own right. Some of the grid-based 'Games with Words' are included in the joint show with Sooster, for example one which translates:

I	am in	love	with
An	na	Mar	kovna
and	she	is in love	with me!

OPPOSITE ABOVE: 'The Man Who Never Threw Anything Away', from Ten Characters, *1981-88, detail; BELOW: 'The Short Man (The Bookbinder)', from* Ten Characters, *1981-88, detail, photos D James Dee; ABOVE: 'Game with Words'*

THE ABSURD AS CONCEPT

PHENOMENA OF HUNGARIAN CONCEPTUALISM
Éva Körner

The twentieth century brought in a time which could be called 'the end of philosophy and the beginning of art'. I do not mean this, of course, strictly speaking, but rather as the 'tendency' of the situation. Certainly, linguistic philosophy can be considered the heir to empiricism, but it's a philosophy in one gear. And there is certainly an 'art condition' to art preceding Duchamp, but its other functions or reasons-to-be are so pronounced that its ability to function clearly as art limits its art condition so drastically that it's only minimally art. In no mechanistic sense is there a connection between philosophy's 'ending' and art's 'beginning', but I don't find this occurrence entirely coincidental. Though the same reasons may be responsible for both occurrences, the connection is made by me. I bring this all up to analyse art's function and subsequently its viability. And I do so to enable others to understand the reasoning of my art and by extension, other artists', as well as to provide a clearer understanding of the term 'Conceptual art'.

In this period of man, after philosophy and religion, art may possibly be one endeavour that fulfils what another age might have called 'man's spiritual needs'. Or, another way of putting it might be that art deals analogously with the state of things 'beyond physics' where philosophy had to make assertions. And art's strength is that even the preceding sentence is an assertion, and cannot be verified by art. Art's only claim is for art. Art is the definition of art.
Joseph Kosuth, 'Art after Philosophy', 1969

Concept art is first of all an art of which the material is concepts . . . Since concepts are closely bound up with language, concept art is a kind of art of which the material is language. That is . . . concept art proper will involve language. From the philosophy of language, we learn that a concept may as well be thought of as the intension of a name; this is the relation between concepts and language . . . If . . . it is enough for one that there be a subjective relation between a name and its intension, namely the unhesitant decision as to the way one wants to use the name, the unhesitant decisions to affirm the names of some things but not others, then *concept is valid language, and concept art has a philosophically valid basis.*
Henry Flynt, 'Concept Art 1961', in *An Anthology*, ed La Monte Young, 1970

The seeing and thinking of the historical man is based on logical contrasts, the seeing and thinking of the archaic man is based on the analogy. The first principle of the analogy is: 'What is down is the very same thing as what is up – what is up is the very same thing as what is down,' says the Tabula Smaragdina

The analogy means that all the phenomena, signs, figures, materials, characters of the world are identical, but that all the phenomena, signs, figures, materials, characters are also different . . .

The mental activity of the modern man is abstract and irreal. The character of the world doesn't lie in the contrasts but in the differences . . .

The formula of the contrast is: the concept and the anti-concept. The two together are the thing itself and its mirror-image. The formula of the difference is: the infinity of the world's similarities and differences . . . All that is similar is different and all that is different is similar, but so that similarity never means entire coincidence and the difference never turns into a total contrast.
Béla Hamvas, *Scientia Sacra 1943-58*, 1988 (accessible to Hungarian artists in the 60s)

It would be possible to quote other ideas that have been the inspiration behind Hungarian conceptualism; these serve only to mark some of the main trends in seeking ways and means. The very core of Hungarian conceptualism was art's existential self-definition. From this point, the fertilised thoughts diverged.

If ever there was a strained situation between the art and artistic thinking of the East and West, then one of the most acute periods was during the 1960s. The end of the decade witnessed an explosion of pent-up tension. A rash of ominous events, such as the circumstances which led to Paris 68 and Prague 68, served to heighten the impact of the spiritual explosion. Curiously, in the West these circumstances spawned a type of art that matured *in isolation from the external world*, rejecting all influence from the outside and absorbed in pure self-definition. It served to embolden artists from the other side of the wall who, unlike their counterparts, *were unable to isolate themselves* from the external world. Instead, these Hungarian artists chose suitable ideas for their liberating goals from the self-purifying act born across the border: there was an inevitable exchange of ideas.

Both East and West were polar opposites in their positions; strategies were neither parallel nor identical. The 'western group' constructed its art as an oxygen tent in a vacuum; the 'eastern group' breathed through filters in a contaminated area. The 'western' influence of conceptualism arrived in Hungary as a type of blood serum used to fill a desperate local shortage. Western and eastern conceptual art are thus two entities of which the former played the dominant, fertilising role, but in the process of gestation the latter deviated from the procreator, assuming specific traits. It repeatedly clarified its mission when specific issues came up but, on the whole, its focus was an elaboration of the intricacies of conceptualism's primary tenets. Contrary to the notion of an 'original' conceptual art, East European conceptual art cannot be described in the clear-cut terms of a dictionary entry. In Hungary, the duty of the artist was to oppose – or side with – the precepts and limits designating each and every level of existence. Western conceptual art played an invaluable role by extending the limits and possibilities of art. In other words, it proposed a type of freedom.

Though primarily inspired by Western conceptual art's *aridity* and autonomy, the 'eastern' variant remained *political* in character, no matter how closely aligned with the Western model. Pure language-orientation as art's self-defining act functioned differently in the East, given that as a political act, it entailed an encroachment upon the artist's personal rights, and in some cases even retaliation – aspects of the practice virtually unknown in the West.

Conceptual art remains influential in Hungary, though from the late 50s, through its peak in '68, on into the 70s, it

was more predominant. Reprisals forcing some to go into exile gave rise to a new situation.

In the West, conceptual art had to struggle against the virulent contemporary avant-garde in which the dominance of a traditional set of genres, especially painting, had to be defended, regardless of any new form it may have assumed. In the East, however, the adversary was not the hegemony of this or that genre, but the all-pervasive tradition-centric attitude, the reference to the classic absolute in which socialist realism enveloped itself, showing off, as it were, in new clothes.

Art used to political ends could survive all the more easily – and indeed has survived to this day – by accepting the standards acknowledged by the great exponents of art history as a shield, a standard which sharply delineated the differences between a traditional 'aesthetic' approach and a reductionist post-Duchampian one. In the 50s these aesthetic standards were still adopted by rebels such as the group hallmarked by Tibor Csernus, who lifted post-naturalism into surrealism, or Béla Kondor, who walked the solitary road of his individual mythology.

As this delineation was being made, the situation became more complex as significant Hungarians emerged from the past or the underground, like for instance Lajos Kassák and Dezso Korniss, who both had survived the temporary reign of social realism. The discovery of an unmarred tradition meant a great deal to the younger generation who were sensitive to conceptual clarity, however incompatible tradition was with the original tenets of conceptual art.

As was noted earlier, Hungarian conceptual art is not identical with the definition, since it defies definition, allowing for some outlines only. The term 'conceptual art' would also include 'project art' and 'play art', both used frequently in Hungary. Project art is a term used by Tamás St Auby, for whom conceptions are propositions on the one hand, which on the other hand take place in processes related to objects. Play art is used in association with István Haraszty, who renders the bizarre contrast between mechanical rationalism and its innate irrationalism.

It is noteworthy that these artists use English terms when defining their practice. One reason for this is the

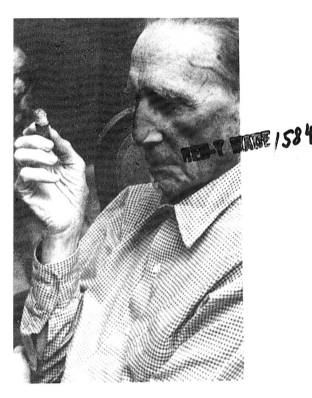

ABOVE: *Gábor Attalai:* Red-y Made, *1970, manipulated Duchamp portrait;* CENTRE: *Gábor Attalai,* Negative Star, *1970, dug out of snow on the Danube quay in Budapest;* BELOW: *Gyula Pauer, 1970,* Pseudo Cube, *aluminium, 34.5x29.5cm*

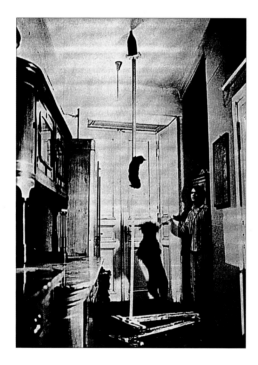

ABOVE: Miklós Erdély, Pinning to the Ceiling, 1971; BELOW: Tamás St Auby, Pinning to the Ceiling, 1971

prevalence of English in the lingo of modern technology, but far more importantly, English is generally considered by the Hungarian public to be alien to art, leaving, as it does for them, the sphere of sensuality and involving mere concepts.

Certainly in Hungary there have never been such conceptual artists *par excellence* as Joseph Kosuth or the Art and Language group. In the East, conceptualism was integrated in the work of sculptors, painters, graphic artists, textile designers, poets, film-makers, performance artists, and even musicians and theatre people, all fraught with the particular problems of their respective disciplines.

In Hungarian conceptual art, Duchamp and Wittgenstein played just as crucial a role as they did for Kosuth. The ready-made and minimal art are of equal significance, but are only rarely important as self-contained statements. It became indispensable for Hungarian conceptual artists to identify points of reference, partly because these then served as points of departure. The ready-made, minimal art, and self-referential statements of Wittgenstein and Kosuth served as some kind of given truths, often inspiring similar statements, often serving as linkages in an exploration of *relations*. The Eastern, hence the Hungarian, conceptual artist was forced to supersede the reductive thesis of truth in and of itself, because he or she could not avoid being confronted with false statements all the time. His or her fundamental task was to formulate a relation to these. The job was made complicated by the fact that the falseness of the statements was not always obvious, often bordering on ambivalence. This job involved self-definition, and the definition of art in a confining social situation and in an existential one.

Since Hungarian conceptual art was not homogeneous, the following examples and phenomena are not generally applicable, referring as they do to individual artists. Only this aggregate of details can suggest a more comprehensive picture.

In addition to Wittgenstein and Kosuth, some conceptual artists were greatly influenced by the transcendental, existential and mythological ideas of a Hungarian thinker little known internationally, Béla Hamvas. His views, including his rejection of the prevalent

pseudo-rationalism, served as examples, as did his life – he wrote his treatises in the Hungarian 'gulag'. Hungarian conceptual artists of totally different outlook and temperament such as Imre Bak, Tamás St Auby, and Tibor Csiky adopted his tenets, each in his own way. The antinomies of early Greek philosophy and the Bible were also influential on account of their inherent interpretative diversity. (These were mainly elaborated on by Miklós Erdély.) György Lukács – though not as positive a figure in the East as he was in the eyes of young intellectuals in the West – served as an alternative to the obligatory, all-pervasive official ideology, and was used as a theme for an ideological game, as in the work of Lázsló Lakner.

To illustrate the difficulty of drawing definitive outlines, as well as to suggest an idea of the enthusiasm permeating these years, a few collective ventures merit attention. Among these is the Copernicus Anniversary in 1971, which set an example for overthrowing the ruling doctrine. This was a university exhibition of young artists who were conceptually involved with 'moving the immovable', or more precisely, the overturning of a monolithic system. Another was the Cobblestone action in 1972, which used the cube as its theme, a 'minimal art' form that was practically banned for its ideological nature which in fact derived from its anti-ideological character. The participants (Gyula Pauer, Gábor Attalai, Tibor Gáyor, Gyula Gulyás and Lázsló Lakner) exploited the material and associational potential suggested by the theme and represented a wide variety of approaches.

From time to time there were less spectacular manifestations of conceptual artists' continual resistance to the official, aggressively influential object cult of commemorative sculpture and historical painting. One target of irony was the particularly schematic output of Dózsa representations, a high-priority theme showing the leader of the Hungarian peasant revolt. Of the many 'interpretations', Dóra Maurer's can be seen as the anticonception to the official conception. The *querying*, *rebellion*, and *irony* implied by the above-mentioned undertakings are notions present throughout Hungarian conceptual art.

There were of course more self-referential manifestations as well, but they are not associated exclusively with any one particular artist, since most artists used several different conceptual approaches. One of these 'pure' self-contained statements is a work – a sentence – by György Jovánovics: 'I wrote each letter of this sentence on another typewriter'. Similar works include the interrelation of Péter Legéndy's sentence and its copy, and St Auby's poems of reduced statements, for example, the following from the 'Will you please' series:

> Imagine
> Finding a long word,
> Finding a short word.
> Cover the long one
>   with the short.

Imre Bak's semantic tautologies and Tibor Csiky's mathematical theories and laws of physics can also be included here.

Just as these foundation-stones were being laid, there arose a new impulse to put into question the nature of reason itself. Jovánovics' sentence 'France's recent king is wise' is a good illustration of this approach. The sentence is linguistically correct, but its meaning is obviously nonsense (France has no king). St Auby's photo *A Budapest aerial photo of an aerial photo of New York* is a slightly different take on the correctness of the statement and the absurdity implied by its conclusion.

St Auby's minimal art objects also belong in this category. Take, for example, *Cooling Water*, which functions only in its 'objective reality', or *A New Unit of Measurement*, a 60-cm-long rod, a self-contained object with associations outside itself. Dates become important here: *Cooling Water* and *A New Unit of Measurement* are dated 1965, following a crucial political year. *New Unit* had associations with police-terror.

Imre Bak's semantically exact works and the references of his word-diagrams dating from the same time should also be mentioned. These draw on the wide references of Eastern philosophy and popular experience, as mediated by Hamvas and Korniss. Csiky's mathematical formulae introduced the notion of a 'soul' into his conceptual framework, while St Auby's pseudo-mathematical formula played with the idea of representational-'non representational'.

Géza Perneczky sought to deflate illusions concerning the concept of 'art'

and expressed his reservations about the possibility of interpretation in the convergence of the words 'yes' and 'no'. Gábor Attalai went back to the source, to Duchamp, when in a tribute to the epoch-making importance of the ready-made, he turned it fully topical. He lifted the word 'red' from 'ready-made' – true, only homonymically – in a witty act of meaning transfer. The symbolism of the colour red should not be lost here. The absurd meeting of the doctrines reinforce, rather than cancel out, each other.

During this time in Hungary important themes were the trap of documentation, the reversibility of exactness, and the arbitrariness of instruments of identification. Endre Tóth's work dealt with the compulsion to define self and world, self and others, and the ironic resolution of this compulsion. Péter Legéndy, as a self-styled 'pseudo-sociologist', wrote questionnaires and collected replies.

As an East European Jewish artist, Janos Major focused on issues of identity and questioned the possibility of an avant-garde and conceptual art in the East European region. Strongly self-ironical and sceptical in tone, he enjoyed pushing similarity and distance to absurd lengths, like 'for example' when he compared himself to his namesake, the world-famous Hungarian-born American, John Neufeld (Major's original name), thus illustrating the differences in possible life-courses in America and Hungary.

István Haraszty's mobiles reference any mechanism senselessly reproducing itself. His system of thought is tied strongly to Eastern Europe. Labelled collectively as 'play art', his contraptions are less self-destructive and less playful than their counterparts in the West. *As a Bird* (1971) consisted of a cage with a live bird inside, suggesting the blocking of all roads to freedom.

Many conceptual works seemed to centre around a term coined by Gyula Pauer whose title 'Pseudo-manifesto' has become almost a household word in Hungary. Dating from 1970, it referred to the absurdity of 'art' and 'artist' in the given situation, and was concerned with the task of removing sediment deposited on concepts and their subsequent reformulation. Pauer translated his thesis into the famous Pseudo-cube. It demonstrated how an exact geometrical figure could be reshaped at will through photographic manipulations.

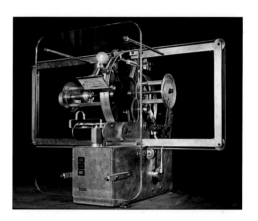

ABOVE: György Jovánovics playing chess with LW, the 'Marionette Extatique', 1970s; CENTRE: István Haraszty, Waiting for Stamping Machine, *early 1980s, mobile date-stamping machine stamping 0s; BELOW: György Jovánovics,* Camera Obscura, *1979*

KARTEI

Georg Lukács
Eigenart des Aesthetischen

MY GEORGE LUKÁCS - BOOK

Lakner László 1970.

ABOVE: *Lászlo Lakner,* My György Lukáks Book, *1970; BELOW: Gyula Pauer,* Forest of Protesting Boards, *1978, Nagyatád*

These ideas also informed film and stage productions at the time. Noteworthy productions from the early 70s include Miklós Erdély's films *Partita* and *Anaxagoras*, St Auby's *Centaur*, and Lázsló Najmanyi's theatre productions (under the pseudonym István Kovacs) *Southern Cross* and *Adventure*. Among other devices, all worked with the associations or disassociations between image and voice-over.

Both Pauer and St Auby made use of hard, contrasting statements. The motto of a St Auby action in 1972 was: 'Everything forbidden is art. Be forbidden'. It was a peculiar form of resistance at a time in Hungary when officially the infamous 'three Ts' *(támogatott* 'promoted', *turt* 'tolerated', *tiltott* 'forbidden') were used to categorise artists. In this relation the tautology of 'forbidden' became reversed in meaning.

Unlike the above-mentioned artists, György Jovánovics did not conceal ambivalences, and instead of giving definitions, he let them float, lifting them into the sphere of poetry where the poetic and the material image correspond at yet another level of ambivalence. His activity focused on the act of loosening in order to reveal hidden traits. He also used unlikely contrasts, like, for example, chess and photography. Chess, as Jovánovics puts it, is one of the most objective games because it precludes cheating. Photography could also be seen in this light, with reference to the quasi-objectivity of the lens. Jovánovics does not, however, bring this up in a conventional, documentary way, but rather tries to capture the ambivalences produced by subsequent reflections or shiftings. What really intrigues him in chess is the notion of concealment, which partly explains his attraction to Farkas Kempelen's chess automaton. With the help of candles and mirrors, Jovánovics was playing with the impulse to turn art immaterial. He associated this with a search beyond the limits of 'official art' and with 'how the eyes of crowned heads could be hoodwinked with the force of spirit' (Jovánovics). His photo series accompanied by Liza Wiathruck's text is a lyrical work about external and internal prohibition, about the space of action. *Camera Obscura* suggests the power of the artist to create an alternative, a virtual picture floating in air. In 1971 Jovánovics staged a joint action with Miklós Erdély, Tamás

St Auby and Lázsló Lakner called *Pinning to the Ceiling*. A spring mechanism forced everyday objects out of their natural places into an absurd situation. The experience of a functionless upside-down system of values was translated into material terms.

Miklós Erdély was the closest to being a conceptual artist *par excellence* in Hungary. Though he was an architect, he often worked with objects, made films and performances, wrote poetry, and painted in later life. His work drew on the ancient Greeks, the Bible, the Oriental sages, and also Einstein and Heisenberg, which made his presence a constant challenge for the Marxist dialecticians. Erdély tried to define things, while still watching the movement unfolding in them. A quote from an early writing of his, 'Dirac in front of the Box-office' helps illustrate this:

1. How is it then? 2. Time and space then. 3. Forget it. 4. The forms of our thinking then. 1. How is that? 2. Forget it. 3. How is it then? 4. Spatialised time, temporalised perception then. 1. Come on, forget it. 2. How is it then? 3. Error has room for everything, or almost everything then . . .

Erdély's solutions always contain counter-arguments as well. His theory of repetition and theory of identity pay close attention to the shifts and traps of definition. Erdély's *Marly Theses* written in 1980 serve as a close here, since they reflect most lucidly Hungarian conceptualism in the 70s.

Marly Theses

* What we regarded as art is a matter of decision, rather than one of definition.

** It makes sense to regard all things which the recognised art forms have in common as art or the essence of art.

** Inversely: the various art forms can be regarded as art precisely because what they have in common is their essence.

*** The greater the diversity of activities and objects regarded as art, the briefer is the list of what they have in common.

*** The more people doing different things are regarded as artists, the less chance there is to find that they have something in common.

* If I decide to regard all the significant representatives of every art form, beginning with prehistoric art right up to modern art, as artists, then I shall be able to find nothing in common in the work of all these people.

** Just because a statement is a matter of decision, it is not necessarily arbitrary.

** Naturally, it is also a matter of decision which artists I regard as significant.

* In my view, an artist is significant if he works towards the effect that the various activities regarded as art should not have anything in common.

* The greatest figures in proper art history are people who did just that.

** In other words, proper art history stripped the word 'art' of its meaning.

*** Since it is not acceptable that a concept (in this case art) can have different meanings on different occasions and since I do not wish to disqualify artists, regarded by me as significant, for the sake of preserving the notion of art (when in fact I regard them as significant precisely because it is due to their work that the notion of art is so elusive), I have to announce that – thanks to the artists – the notion of art is empty, it has no operand and is void of meaning.

* Obviously, the meaning of arbitrary and conventional signs narrows down when the domain of their operands is extended.

* The domain of operands must be specified in order to be able to insure the function of the operator.

* The meaning of non-arbitrary signs – signs which are based on analogies and interaction (iconic or indexical types) – is extended by increasing the domain of their operands.

* If a work of art is a sign, then it is of this type.

** In the case of the arbitrary and conventional signs, their operands must have something in common; by contrast, the other type of signs invoke all the possible – and at times fundamentally different – features of their operands themselves.

*** This is the reason why [a non-arbitrary sign] can become a multivocal 'supersign', with a tendency to expand into infinity.

* The meaning of a work of art is not the total sum of its different references; rather, a work of art makes these references possible, or otherwise, it virtually contains them.

** Because of its analogous and interactive references, a work of art might mean one thing here and another there according to the actual period or environment; or it might even mean both things at the same time.

*** While in the case of conventional signs their meaning narrows down as the domain of their operands increases, in the case of iconic/indexical type of signs polysemy might lead to the fading and devaluation of the signs, and ultimately to complete emptiness even,

as it often happens with works of art.

**** A work of art, therefore, can be regarded as a sign which enhances any one of the various meanings at the expense of the rest: it multiplies them or it uses one to cancel out another by destructive interference, thus making it impossible for the work of art as a whole to have a meaning.

***** Such a sign should not be thought analogous with 'x', the algebraic independent variable able to assume an arbitrary value; a work of art cannot assume any meaning, except when it is misinterpreted.

* Roughly speaking, the various meanings appear on four different levels:

– Thematic level (what)

– Technical level (how)

– In an art historical context (with reference to every work of art produced by old and contemporary artists), further broken down as:

– what

– how

– In a social, historical context (set against the social and cultural background, which can be narrower or broader, depending on the artist's qualities), further broken down as:

– what

– how

** The interference of the various meanings mostly follows from the vertical interblending of the four levels.

*** The montage effect represents the references that destructively interfere with each other within any one of the levels (together with the inevitable modulated meanings of the other levels).

* In a manner of speaking, a work of art is filled with invalidated meanings, and as such, it works as a meaning-repellant.

* The message of a work of art is its inherent emptiness.

** It is this emptiness that the receptive mind receives.

*** The work of art makes room in the receptive mind, when its message is 'understood'.

**** The recipient then says: 'nice', which is another empty statement.

***** Then comes the feeling of freedom, which is nothing else than emptiness, space in the train of 'recognised necessity': a place.

****** A place: for the not-yet-realised.

* By discussing the things in life, a work of art makes these things disappear.

* By discussing the things in life, a work of art makes discussion on these things disappear.

Miklós Erdély, Lecture given at the conference 'Art in a Changing World', 1980

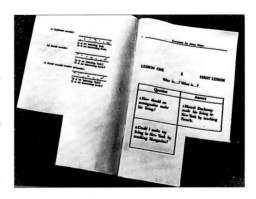

ABOVE: János Major: My First Grammar Book, *1970; BELOW: Tamás St Auby,* Cooling Water, *1965, bottle containing warm water that is replaced once cold, photo by the artist*

CONTEMPORARY POLISH ART

AN INTERPRETATION AND ANALYSIS
Paulina Kolczynska

Certificate of Belonging:
Figurative painting in Poland during the 1980s

During the 1970s in Poland experimental activity of a conceptual origin was related to autonomous artistic searching. This involved, as Dorota Monkiewicz puts it, 'objective techniques of the structure of the picture like photography, video, where the whole focus has been upon the possibilities of the media'. The aim was simple – to enrich objective visual language free from aesthetic prejudices.[1] This also helped to develop interesting ideas in the sphere of post-avant-garde film during the 1970s and 1980s. In Poland avant-garde formations formulated many outstanding ideas, starting with the concrete poetry and the Office of Poetry established by Andrzej Partnum where changes of emphasis in the text from its verbal meaning towards visual values, opened a new chapter. Simultaneously Anastazy Wisniewski had been involved in openly structured action at the Repassage Gallery in Warsaw; and the paratheatrical action of Tadeusz Kantor at Gallery Krysztofory in Cracow and at the Cricot-2 theatre in 1970 had also been developing to become one of the most spectacular contributions towards universal values in contemporary art.

Art was growing directly from art; from thinking about art, from experimental values, and from speculation on the value of artistic ideas. Discussions concerning the artistic object itself were rooted in ideas of conceptual art, fluxus and performance, where an important role was played by the semantics of concrete and meta-artistic poetry. All the artistic approaches defined loosely by Ryszard Wasko as 'postconstructivist trends'[2] have placed Polish contemporary art on the same line as broad developments in Western art. The importance of this art and its achievement were shown in the massive exhibition 'Construction in Process', which was in Lodz in 1981 and in Munich in 1985. This exhibition exemplified the need to participate in the life of society according to the constructivist motto expressed by Szczuka that 'the artist can not be a ain ornament of the society, the artist must cooperate in the organisation of life'. In spite of spectacular success in showing the wholeness of the development of independent art in Poland, and in building cooperative ties between Western and Eastern artists, the avant-garde formations faced major obstacles during the years of Martial Law, which saw the closure of the alternative exhibition spaces and galleries. Due to the structure and aims of this type of art, there was a significant lack of what Henry Stażewski described as: 'Negation or approval of phenomena taking place in the reality called – modernity'. Meta-artistic discussion concerning the work of art itself was no longer sufficient in confrontation with the needs and atmosphere of Polish society.[3] The established order demanded a highly defined artistic language and fully readable artistic signs. But the *real* situation demanded changes which the older generation could not answer because of an overall crisis of the avant-garde, struggling with a lack of innovative vision. The crisis of the avant-garde in Poland had strong parallels in Western Europe, where widely understood problems of 'artistic autonomy, status of the work of art and principles of creative action' needed to be revived in order to create new structures. Poland was a stage of endless discussions and uncertainty concerning the possibility of creation after conceptual and media art.[4] Phenomena of a non-artistic nature such as the establishment of the free trade union Solidarity and the tragedy of Martial Law made a great impact on art after 1983. Younger artist newly graduated or still at the Fine Arts Academy did not hesitate to set aside avant-garde paradigms in order to respond more directly to events. The national tragedy

Zbigniew Libera, The Bather (Le Baigneur), 1991, plexiglas, rubber, aluminium, TV-set, VHS conductors, kinescope lamp, photo Mikolaj Malinowski

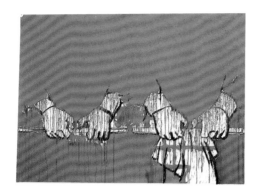

Włodzimierz Pawlak, Breaking of the Glass Tubes, *1987, oil, 135x185cm, photo Anna Pietrzak-Bartos*

of Martial Law demanded an artistic reaction with the capacity to do full justice to the present. An artistic will to free itself from the abstract tradition and cosmopolitan forms dominated and became the major factor in new painterly developments. This also involved a return to traditional media and traditional studio practices, which assigned a primacy to the subjective factor (meaning the subject *as* factor). 'Revived' painting found its stylistic articulation in figurative and expressive works by J Beres, E Arendt-Sobocka, W Obrzydowski and the Wprost group. Development of figurative painting in Poland, indeed, came almost at the same time as similar revivals in Germany (Neue Wilde) and Scotland (Glasgow Pups), but somewhat later than Italian 'Arte cifra', French 'Figuration libre' or 'New Image Painting' from America.

In Poland its most representative manifestation was Gruppa from Warsaw, whose first appearance as a group was in 1983. In the words of Ryszard Stanisławski, 'in spite of crisis and forced by the circumstances of political break-offs, culture maintained its rhythm of development'.[5] In the case of Poland, and of Gruppa in particular, this is shown through the German scholarship work of Jaroslaw Modzelewski and Marek Sobczyk, and the influence (especially on Sobczyk) of older artists such as E Mucha (as T Boruta has pointed out).[6] Original work and discussion concerning present events and narrative style became inseparable. Young artists managed to escape from the pressures of events towards self-realisation and a dynamic of imaginative development.

Escape was possible thanks to a systematic reappraisal of studio practices by the artists themselves. Ryszard Grzyb, a member of Gruppa, said in 1983: 'Painting does not restrict itself to the problems of composition and colour. Painting just this is something undescribable and absurd. If someone's occupation is as a painter then that is an absurd man in this country and in this time'.[7] A distancing from conventional artistic action opened up new fields of thought which Woźniak described as a deprivation of painting from its classic elements. In other words the opening of new semantic and aesthetic perspectives became the main way of answering the problems of artist and viewer. In many cases (as Piotr Krakowski ob-

served) religious and patriotic subjects were mythologised and radicalised in a specific way. 'Irony, tragic and at the same time comic and paradoxical discussions, paintings on paper, ephemera, drawings and ludic actions became the main means of artistic expression.[8]

In the case of paintings, 'Territory-Poland' was the starting point of the individual observations, judgements and reinterpretations. Figures free from ideological notions and Utopias became the means of articulation. In order to achieve truthfulness of figure and sign, young independent painters attempted a widespread re-evaluation in the difficult fields of culture, religion and Polish history. Thanks to the ratification of these cultural spheres, they managed to grasp hidden mechanisms and structures ruling outer and inner reality. It is also worth mentioning that even though artists worked strongly within their time, and the frames of their activity were drawn by the space (territory) in which they worked, they also, nevertheless, retained some independence from this framework. The means to this involves mixing layers of artistic ideas with religious and ethical references, so that their paintings not only mirrored reality but also twisted it. In Sobczyk, works with religious metaphors are confronted by strong sexual allusion. By emphasising ridiculous aspects of reality (with an element of dismissiveness and simplification of figure) the artist more than underlines his non-conformist approach towards the existing state of values in Poland. Multi-figure and multi-zone iconography with condensed rhetoric exceeded and subverted the space of reality. Sobczyk built a more universal world through communicated truths which exceeded the privacy of the individual and at the same time inspired a belief in the reality of post-Martial Law Poland.

Symbols of Christianity and unexpected associations appeared also in the paintings of Ryszard Grzyb and Ryszard Woźniak. Woźniak operates with metaphors of sign and figure shown in gestures and ironic representations, but in this case the political context has been mixed with symbolic archetypes. Grzyb in his iconography bridges social and political commentary with religious elements where folk motifs, masks and simple eroticism build a very straightforward language. 'Figures mean what they represent'[9] and important elements of dismissiveness articulate a strong criticism of Polish society, pointing out both its faults as well as more general human failings. A second important field of rhetorical painterly discussion (as mentioned earlier) addresses history. Works by Grzyb and Kowalewski undertake an interpretation of historic themes from the point of view of the relations between history, tradition, and everyday life. The style of Kowalewski has been described by Anda Rottenberg as 'painfully simple and defencelessly pure painterly language'.[10] Historic problems and confrontations with political realities are presented with a directness and unambiguity which shocks the viewer.

Diagnosis of the material and spiritual state of the country has also been conducted in a language which, in its privacy and relaxed attitude, affirms a kind of artistic independence from outer realities.

This can be seen in the works of Modzelewski, who accumulates meaningless figures and emblematic signs where ill-defined gestures and abstract details chase after real phenomena. Doubled-up forms also serve here as strengthening figures. Their echoes support what Paul Ricoeur calls the figure's ability to 'overcome the silence, overcome growing amnesia with the use of empty signs' – like empty words when values have been questioned.

Articulation of the figure has become centrally important in the Polish context: 'To see the cruel and fascinating face of the world – or to see the mask and understand that we are equal elements of its totality. Stripped from our skin to the same degree as stripping (others), equally hidden as revealed.'[11] This guilt and the responsibility for addressing and articulating social and moral problems are central concerns of Wlodzimierz Pawlak. His art works have been built on emergence and disappearance in a field of sketchy figures. Contrary to Sobczyk, Pawlak's figures are not repainted, they are painted over. Destroyed gesture functions as a perfect metaphor for what was described earlier as the mystery of the 'equally hidden and revealed' truth of the reality. Self-destructive gesture here affirms the importance of signs on the walls of Polish cities which had been painted over by the authorities during Martial Law. Symbolic expressions of destruction and auto-profanation are

also signals of a negative approach towards the order of outer reality. The destroying gesture becomes a sign of time . . . references to the substance of this gesture generalise the specific historic time from which they come. This gesture can be seen as a form of very strong protest against thoughtless violence in the general human dimension. A bond with present modernity is also shown by paintings on paper which enable the artist to 'grasp the spontaneity of time'. Painting on paper has here acquired a very special meaning. Firstly it was innovative through being introduced by the aforementioned Modzelewski and Gruppa after their visit to Germany. Secondly it supported the general climate of destruction and the courage of admitting nonsense and affirming the unimportance of the art object itself. (Pawlak actually encouraged the viewers to walk on his painted papers at the Dziekanka Gallery.) This type of creativity also underlines a relationship with the post-avant-garde art and surrounding discussion. The strength of young artists lies in a strong voice which beaks through politics and artistic borders. The most important aspect of this is the style worked out by Gruppa based on strategies of auto-irony, shocking effects and dismissiveness which were very valuable artistic tools in the face of the moral destruction wrought by Martial Law. Thanks to these tools artists survived the pressure of society and reality. This ironic dimension revealed reality without creating tiresome ambiguity. It 'killed its mask' and gave a meaning to the figure.[12] Ironic formulae of laughter and scream can be associated with the power of painterly stylistics, 'because the scream is recognised as a form of laughter, and laughter (with its origin in the joke) becomes a form of anxiety'.[13] This full articulation of anxiety and fear has been shown with maturity in the paintings of Gruppa, as a universal criticism of present times. They also make possible the invasion of a new artistic truth, which bridges the remaining gap between 'picture and logos'.

Finally it could be said that the most important general achievement of Gruppa lies in the ability to find fresh stylistic and rhetorical formulae which locate the bond between artwork and territory in historical and sociological analysis. Finally there is a great mani-

Włodzimierz Pawlak, Sterile Container under the Control of the Authorities, *1985, paint on packing paper, 195x204cm, photo Anna Pietrzak-Bartos*

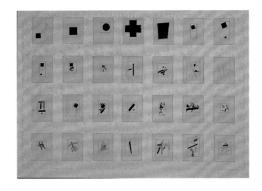

festation of individuality which is supported by a search for personal truth in the specific conditions of heroic times in Poland. Their work shows a mature artistic articulation of reality.

Intermezzo

'The Heroic years are over,' said Magdalena Tarabula, director of the Zderzak Gallery in Cracow. Reality post-1989 brought many changes of organisation and financial structures. The needs and character of artistic society have completely changed.

This is shown especially by the relations between official exhibition spaces and artists. Boycotts of official exhibition spaces and revolts against authority have become history. First signs of normalisation came with the possibility of producing far-reaching publicity, free art promotion and the giving of rights to private and alternative galleries. Today's situation is far from fully stabilised because economic changes and free market laws have affected culture. Problems (this time of a financial nature) have become a dire source of affliction to galleries.

Gallery Foksal at the end of 1992-93 faced closure (due to the high rent), but thanks to the petitions of friends of this famous exhibition space (from Poland, France and Germany) it has been saved. Many other galleries of less importance have not managed to survive. Despite this, the gallery landscape has maintained and developed many levels of interest from galleries (such as Zacheta) dependent on the Ministry of Culture and Art with a coherent programme approved by the Ministry to the gallery of the Union of the Artists – *ZPAP na Mazowieckiej* – and galleries of the BWA, or private galleries like Appendix in Warsaw, Stawski in Cracow, Anna Karenska in Poznan or Gallery Asik in Bydgoszcz.

Many exhibition spaces such as Gallery Dziekanka from Warsaw or Zderzak from Cracow (established in 1985) continue a healthy tradition of art promotion based on programmes built over the years. Other centres are also open towards international cooperation supporting the best traditions of Polish contemporary art and showing it as part of the European dimension. A newly created centre for contemporary art, State Gallery Sopot (director Ryszard Ziarkiewicz) started dynamic activity in collecting, and exhibiting art works

within the post-conceptual mode. The most notable exhibition which has taken place recently is : 'Perserweracja mistyczna i Roza', which gathered together the youngest Polish artists and introduced German artists as well. International contacts generate interesting projects with very high standards of publication and presentation. Noteworthy in this respect is the exhibition of Polish contemporary art, 'Polen Kunst Zeit' (1990), supported by Adenauer Foundation from Germany with the cooperation of the director of the Appendix gallery, Pawel Sosnowski, and the former director of the Museum of art in Lodz, Ryszard Stanislawski. A Polish dimension was also present at the Chicago International Art Exposition in 1992 when Stawski from Cracow cooperated with the Lakeside Group from Chicago. There are many interests and types of art supported by the galleries, but the existence of these centres depends, of course, on the managerial and curatorial skills of the people working there. Lack of financial back up in this sector is very pronounced, and the network of formal and informal institutions supporting art promotion and culture in general is not yet well developed. The first years of decentralisation did not arrive with sufficient information on promotional activities relating to the visual arts. There are some new institutions with independent sources of money, and these are helping to secure promotional development. Notable in this respect is the Centre for Contemporary art supported by the Open Society Foundation of George Soros and the Centre for Contemporary Art in Warsaw (Zamek Ujazdowski) and the Centre for Polish sculpture in Oronsko, which both support experimental artists.

Changes are visible, but financial barriers and an undeveloped art market slow down the promotional process.[14] At the level of the non-profit-making galleries, finances present the same problem. From the artist's point of view it is possible to say in general that there are still not enough good galleries and not enough curators or exhibition organisers.

This intermezzo works as a threshold between two eras. Looking back it is important to say that there are few active possibilities for developing far-reaching initiatives in relation to international circles.

Włodzimierz Pawlak, ABOVE: Malevich (monochromatic), *1992, oil, 135x190cm; OPPOSITE:* Malevich (colour), *1992, oil, 135x190cm*

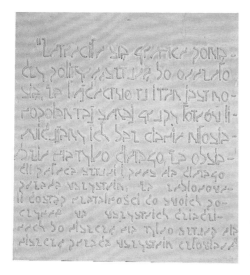

Włodzimierz Pawlak, Alphabet of Strzeminski,
1991, oil, 130x120cm

Turning the page of the history it is important to mention the positive aspect of Poland's recent past, which was defined by Hans Gunter Golinski, who said, 'The imposed isolation of the country [created] an intimacy of the artist, critics and the public which can be really envied'.[15]

It is not possible to say this looking at the art world in Poland today. What has happened under the new conditions can best be described as a kind of dispersal of the art world. The art market remains nascent. Paintings tend to be bought directly from the artist rather than from the gallery. Many galleries (in order to improve their financial situation) introduce selling points which tend to deform the character of the exhibition space. At this level, the free market rather than the art world has had most influence in forming the atmosphere of the gallery interior. What is really needed to build, support and protect the overall standard of culture is for the visual arts to find devoted curators who will give special attention to art of a high standard. What is also needed is for promoters to take risks and support young artists, giving them the opportunity to present their ideas on an international level. It is this art which will soon produce the vision of the 1990s where the rhythm of motifs planted in the present will find its continuation. The stylistics and rhetorics of this art are the source of many discussions today when the artistic scene has been occupied by established artists (who made their debuts after Martial Law) and young artists who have not yet fully defined their visual language.

A second sphere of discussion concerns the renewal and development of those meta-artistic languages that make possible the interpretation and diagnosis of contemporary art. Art and its production are once more closely examined, through the changing of the surrounding context in which their values function. The intermezzo concerning art must finish soon so that an appropriate set of tools to deal with the new philosophies can be fabricated.

Artists – Philosophers
Poetry of the 'empty sign'. In search of the individual artistic language in Polish art of the 1990s

The post-1989 era has brought interesting stylistic changes amongst those artists who started their careers after 1983. The new turn has been marked by the far-reaching consequences of abandoning figuration.

The changing of the rhetoric of the sign, and the changing of artistic preferences from the figurative towards the abstract (on the one hand) and from the form of painterly articulation towards three-dimensional objects (on the other) prepare the ground for a new artistic perception.

It is worth mentioning here that a preference for one style does *not completely* exhaust and silence the abandoned stylistic motifs. These can come back to life along with the artistic philosophy which they mirror. Renewal of the formal and visual language from the figurative towards the category of the 'empty sign' [16] has meant the up-dating of the structural and conceptual interests begun in 1960-70 by previously mentioned circles of the post-avant-garde.

'Polish artists are exhausted with political questions.'[17] They have gone back into art, as Anda Rottenberg puts it; going back into art coincides with the important political changes comparable to regaining sovereignty in the international area. This external condition provides at the same time lots of 'psychological space' which can be used by the artist without ballasts of obligation or 'nihilistic anarchy and national martyrdom'.[18] In the 1990s the normalisation of everyday life provides a return to the search for conceptual features, but, in fact there are also discussions in terms of the object of art itself where the biggest space is given over to the artist. This is because the artist is still able to concentrate on himself and to search for new forms from the viewpoint of the 'credibility of himself towards himself'.[19]

The influence of the physical territory will appear only through the transformations of the philosophy of the object, because the experience of the media obliterates local or regional ties through the universal and the international visual language of contemporary art.

A philosophy, which today inspires and, at the same time, is being questioned as a source of new ideas is that of Strzeminski (the idea of the unistic picture) and the structure of universal time in art. Other sources of discussion lie in the constructivist tradition transformed in the 1960s in the light of the philosophy of reduction and early proto-conceptual motifs of thinking in the works of Opalka and Winiarski Gierowski.

The empty sign 'has become the sign of an extensive revision of theoretical and pragmatic foundations' (Zbigniew Dlubak, *Art Beyond the World of Meaning*[20]) and, also opens up the possibility of constructing contemporary art with a strong notion of avant-garde artifact structure where dualities based on ontic . . . structural and semantic composition allow unique 'inner theory making, which is a parallel to artistic discussion' (Ryszard Kluszczynski).[21]

Włodzimierz Pawlak leads this kind of artistic discussion with a painterly language. His return to a silent visual field has been marked by the reduction of narrative and dynamic features. Multilayered white pictures open up monotonous lines of black dashes. These works are, in fact, called *The Diary*. The artist aims to discuss a mode of timelessness where the picture lasts within itself. Layers of white paint and rhythms of black dashes in the case of *Diary* or the three-dimensional inscription from the unreadable alphabet of Strzeminski in the picture of the same title (*Alphabet of Strzeminski*) also introduce experiences of the proto-picture. Here 'timelessness' and an 'over spatial' construction of the visual field regulate 'the stream of the coincidental, without meaning appearances and disappearances (of the objects)'.[22] The most interesting element is some kind of pre-historic starting point, where time itself is at its beginning, leaving all possibilities of creation and fulfilment in the picture open from the start. A different perspective is introduced by reference to the visual language of Malevich. The doctrine of 'reaching the summit of true unmasked art and of bringing 'true feeling' has been given new dimension. Idea becomes a question rather than answer and is directed towards a new construction of the visual field. By the use of suprematist language in one picture Pawlak shows a whole spectrum of images from the cubo-futuristic period of Russian painting. The creation of

'horror vacui' – the mixing and density of images and symbols – leads to a neutralisation of the original meaning of the individual images. It also constructs a new context where symbols may become ornament or may provide a notion of space where individual measurements for meaning and time find an easy place.

'Empty sign' becomes the feature of individual time, time in the dispersal wherein exists the possibility of artistic dialogue between the artist and the object. Kazuo Katase in 1982 observed that 'art is not for others at the beginning, it's for ourselves'. This intimate dialogue supports the factor of search and development and becomes a part of the inspiration on the way to the artist's definition of spiritual space. This tendency is visible in the sculptures and installations of Pawel Althamer.

Works shown in 1991 in Warsaw called *Lodz* (Boat), which present an iron, horizontal human-sized object, began this special tendency. The artist closed himself within the object and by lying in it, was surrounded and restructured spatially by the work of art he had himself created. The artwork as an object with individuality offered to the artist/viewer by the restricted space thereby also offered a different perspective on both the perception of the world and itself.

This physical interiority of the object can also be seen as an 'announcement' of the exploration of the interiority of the artist himself. This step was most fully realised in 1993 in the installation called *Dark Chamber*. The inner spiritual space became a field of exploration. The recognition and peace found within himself by the artist/viewer comes from darkness and the totality of self. Darkness also functions here as the reversed inner space of the individual, which bares the sign of oneness.

Amongst all these philosophical motifs there is another challenge which is visible in the sculptures oriented towards the 'wide post-Beuys tradition' of Mirosław Bałka. Specific poetry and a philosophy of the materials offers a description of the individual world. A subtle dialogue takes place in the objects where steel and salt or tinted wood, iron and sponge with salty water co-exist as components in one construction. Dialogue in some cases changes into a whisper which does not need to accommodate space. Therefore the

objects seem to diminish and inner relations have more weight than interaction with the outerworld. The primarily inner dialogue is also enriched by the interference of human presence. An awareness of this presence serves to make the object more approachable. This happened with the objects presented in the Polish Pavilion at the 1993 Venice Biennale in the exhibition *37.1.*

In the piece entitled *367x224x255,* 1993 the artist used pieces of soap. As remains of human presence, they were invested with a kind of existential shiver. They became, thereby, a challenge to reality through the stigma of resembling objects outside art. 'Dialogue with material works as a kind of liaison with reality where 'saved remains of history bring back the private and individual dimension in dealing with time and space (A Przywara).[23]

In this case the significance of the 'being' of the object has been underlined by the relation with reality.

Different artistic and philosophical approaches are visible in the works of Zbigniew Libera whose works were introduced by Helena Kontova at the Aperto at the 1993 Venice Biennale. These art objects are based on spiral and sinusoidal constructions from plexiglass and aluminium. The function of these structures is to enable the work through rhythmic energisation of shape to produce a transformation. The audio-visual part of the work (supported by clinically clean construction of the tubes) announces the inseparable dependency of these elements (eg T*he Bather,* 1991). This sound and picture became a part of the construction. *The Bather* involves a cyclic elapse of the sound of dripping water vanishing into empty plexiglass tubes. It is a metaphor for the deceased human being (described by workers in funeral parlours as *le bagneur* – the bather).

The human association comes through the water's sound being freed by the construction. Its specific music and the shiny clearness of the object evokes the hospital interior, where the sound of life-support machines echoes the heart. The drama of the situation has been frozen, emotions put aside. The structure of the objects serves as both producer and container of a power which in case of *The Segment of the Signal,*

1993, aims to describe the thin red line between life and death by objects which evoke 'life' more than the human itself.

The deep metaphors and sophisticated language of Libera opens a very original field where, in silence fractured by sound, the artist opens an area where the 'independence of the human system' is vividly questioned.

All these examples serve as underlying means for diagnosing the state of post-conceptual art, and also as symptoms of that relation between society and artist where the distance grows even wider due to the problems and preoccupations of today's world. But their power lies in breaking through to new artistic fields. Their major achievement may be described as lying in their contribution to universal culture and a set of values based on continuation and innovation within the post-Duchamp and post-Beuys tradition of media. The implications and development of this visual language and parallel problematics may be very significant for 'the ability to make judgements' concerning the condition of culture and human being, so much awaited in public contemporary art.

The second achievement can be seen in a sustained (although transformed) bond which can be loosely described as 'with the territory of origin' on philosophical and aesthetic levels. Both components achieve a significant balance within the art object.

There is no doubt that public interest in contemporary art in for example, Poland is not sufficient, there is also no doubt that what has already been emerging will have a strong impact on continuing artistic creation into the 1990s and beyond.

Art itself has an important capacity, which conditions the progress of humanity the power of 'relating and separating people'. This should not be underestimated. Therefore information about ideas, development and international interaction, seems to be more valuable than ever in the light of the changes in Central and Eastern Europe. It is hoped, therefore, that the discussion and examples offered here, bring about a greater understanding of the artistic problems and artistic solutions found in this part of Europe.

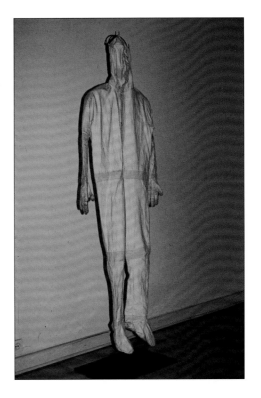

Paweł Althamer, ABOVE: The Boat, *1991, linen, approx 2m; OPPOSITE:* The Boat, *1991, metal, approx 2m, photos Rafal Szambelan*

Notes

1 Dorota Monkiewicz, *O scenie artystycznej w Polsce, Unvollkommen Die aktuelle Kunstszene in Polen* (On the artistic stage in Poland, not perfect today's artistic stage in Poland), catalogue, Museum Bochum, 1993.

2 Interview with Ryszard Wasko before the exhibition 'Construction in Process', Lodz, 1981.

3 Henryk Stażewski, 'Theory and Praxis', in *Miejse sztuki* (Place of Art), 1975.

4 Ryzsard Kluszczynksi, *Kino w diasporze: Avant garda filmowa w Polsce in lat siedemdziesiatych i osiemdziesiatych in Oko i Ucho Problemy sztuk wizualnych i sluchowych* (Cinema in diaspora: The film avant-garde of the 70s and 80s in *Eye and Ear, problems of the visual and audio visual arts*), Lodz, 1989, p8.

5 Ryszard Stanislawski, *Z muzealnej praktyki odpowiedz na postawione pytania in Kolekcja sztuki 20 wieku, Muzeum sztuki w Lodzi* (From the museum practice, answers on posed question in the collection of the 20th-century art, Lodz Art Musem), Warsaw, 1991, p37.

6 Tadeusz Boruta transcribed in *Art and Business* 3/4, 1993, p65.

7 Interview with Gruppa, Odpowiedzi czlonkow Gruppy na trzy pytania Z Kwiatkowskiego 1983, *Gruppa 1982-1992, catalogue,* Galeria Zacheta, Warsaw, 1992, p58.

8 Piotr Krakowski, 'Dwurnik's life-long war, Zdersk Gallery Cracow', in *Art and Business* 7/8, 1992, p34.

9 Anda Rottenberg, 'Wstep do Katalogue' in *Gruppa 1982-1992*, catalogue, Galeria Zacheta, Warsaw, 1992, p58.

10 Ibid.

11 Ryszard Grzyb, *W parku na rzece. Oj dobrze juz nr 7* (in the park, by the river. How good yet no 7), 1988, ibid.

12 J Brach, 'Czaina Wstep do katalogu' (introduction to the catalogue), op cit.

13 Ryszard Grzyb, *Oj dobrze juz nr 1* (How good yet no 1), 1984.

14 Interview with Ryszard Wasko before the exhibition 'Construction in Process', Lodz, 1981.

15 Hans Gunter Golinski, *'Unvollkommen Kunst als Reflexion des Nicht-konnes'* (Not perfect art as the reflection on inability), *Unvollkommen Die Aktuelle Kunstszene in Polen*, Museum Bochum, 1993.

16 Zbigniew Dlubak, *Sztuka poza swiatem znaczen* (Art beyond the world of meaning, paper for the conference on the contextual art), CAEC Toronto, 1976.

17 Kim Levin, 'Warsaw, Poland', in *Sculpture* March-April 1993.

18 Kazimierz Piotrowski, op cit no 10.

19 Maria Morzuch Trwanie in *Oko i Ucho* (*Eye and Ear* magazine), p36, Lodz, 1989.

20 Op cit no 18.

21 Op cit no 6.

22 Op cit no 3.

23 Andrzej Przywara 'Puste miejsce' (Empty place), in Mirosław Bałka, *April/My body cannot do everything I ask for*, Galeria Foksal, Warsaw, 1991.

Zbigniew Libera, Segment of the Signal, *1993, aluminium, oscilloscope lamp, circuit generating chaos, plexiglas, generator of the function, photo Grzegorz Olech*

MIROSŁAW BAŁKA

WILLIAM FURLONG AT THE POLISH PAVILION
With Anda Rottenberg and Anna Kamachora

William Furlong: Mirosław, could you first of all describe the works you have installed in this pavilion?

Mirosław Bałka: It is not easy to explain in words, because it is a very big installation. It consists of three parts so it is a kind of triptych; the first part is the corridor, which is eight metres long and 160 centimetres wide; the walls are three metres high and they are covered with a thin coat of grey soap to a level of 190 centimetres, which is my height. The soap is the cheapest soap you can get. This belt of soap on two sides leads you into the space, which is divided into two parts, left and right. My intention was to come first into the left part, which is more active. The works are made from steel that has been touched by the weather a little bit so there are signs of rust; the other materials I use are an artificial carpet which is turned upside down, some small pieces of used soap, steel rope and two trash cans. So this is a very active part of this exhibition. Then when you see the right part it is more peaceful; it is very horizontal and consists of the terrazzo plate and heat and ash.

WF: You have described the works physically but can you now elaborate on the idea of scale in the installation?

MB: The main size in this exhibition is the size of the floor, of the kitchen in my studio which I use as a model and it is repeated in three moments, the first time time represents a flood, the second is the form for something, and the third is just a body.

Anna Kamachora: I wrote in the catalogue that in a way your work is related to the average temperature of the human body. The title of your installation is *37.1*; how is this related to your work?

MB: The normal temperature is 37, so this extra .1 has the rather symbolic meaning of being like the first step into a fever or like the last step out of a fever. This was the meaning of the title. I think that here the temperature is much higher because of the temperature outside.

AK: Anda, could you tell me something about why you have chosen Mirosław Bałka for the Polish Pavilion. Is it because his work is representative of the current situation in Poland?

Anda Rottenberg: In real art we can't speak about current situations. Situation describes the average, and I would rather stress the quality of art as the main consideration in choosing Mirosław, with whom I have worked for over eight years. I have followed every step of his development as an artist and I was convinced from the very beginning that he is really a very serious artist, one who may make a real impact on the international art scene. The intention is not to represent the country; the intention is to let the artist make a real piece of art to be seen by the whole world, and my conviction is very simple: Mirosław Bałka is simply a very good artist and that is why he is here.

WF: The issue was raised about the relationship between the political characteristics of Poland and your selection, and you seem to be saying that you weren't particularly concerned; but can you talk a little bit about Mirosław's work in relation to the context, because there must be some links.

AR: I have to come back to the beginning of his activity because he started his work as a independent artist in the mid 80s, when we had martial law. It was a very strange situation because Poland was divided into two parts. One part was official and the other, which was the majority, was unofficial. Poland was in a state, let's say, of disease which lasted and lasted, and of course artists took part in the opposition, resurrection if you like, but this kind of personal involvement of artists in politics couldn't last for ever. Our country hasn't gone the same way towards independence as the rest of the Eastern Bloc. We were the first to be, let's say, avant-garde. I don't want to exaggerate, but we started long before, so we were pretty tired in the mid 80s, and one can feel from the artist's work that he didn't want to engage in the fight against the system any more, but because there was permanent fighting all around, in a way one couldn't avoid it.

For example, Mirosław's early works were of course in opposition to both the underground church movement and to the official movement. He raised up the very personal point of view in a way which in my view was more than just an artistic statement. It was an attitude towards politics. Politics cannot interfere in art. That is why I would say there is a very specific relationship between politics and the generation of artists who started in the 80s. There were a lot of very ironic manifestations in which Mirosław participated, like the mirror in the circus, reflecting some official problems or habits in the field of art. For example he and the group he belonged to or established did performances or exhibitions for the benefit of, for example, the 1st of May as well as for New Year's Eve, Easter and Women's Day. All this points to the sociological and cultural circumstances he was working in. What he is now doing also refers to those levels, but the language has changed. Of course his personal experience is deeper because it is longer. It is probably more serious than it was at the beginning, but the attitude doesn't change much.

WF: Does Mirosław want to say anything about these issues.

MB: think it is a very good explanation. I have nothing to add.

Anda Rottenberg was the Polish curator and selector of Mirosław Bałka for the Polish Pavilion and Anna Kamachora is an art critic from Bratislava. The interview was included in Audio Arts Magazine, *Venice Biennale 1993, vol 13 nos 2 & 3. William Furlong,* Audio Arts: Definitions of Practice, *will be published by Academy Editions in July 1994.*

OVERLEAF: Mirosław Bałka, 37.1, installation in the Polish Pavilion at the Venice Biennale, 1993

LACAN AND ŽIŽEK

AN INTRODUCTION
Paul Crowther

At the end of the 20th century, the writings of Jacques Lacan are proving of seminal importance in relation to the understanding of many aspects of art, and culture generally. Lacan's own oeuvre is a formidably difficult one. The difficulty does not arise from any infelicities of style, but rather from a surplus of stylistic strategies and quirks. For the fundamental point of Lacan's understanding of the human reality, is that this reality is profoundly elusive, and not amenable to systematic articulation in any absolute sense.

Lacan's influence has been significantly developed of late through the work of Slavoj Žižek. In particular, Žižek's recent book *Looking Awry: An Introduction to Jacques Lacan Through Popular Culture* (MIT Press, 1991) has attracted great interest through showing something of the broadness of scope and applicability of Lacanian thought. In the paper 'The Enlightenment in Laibach' (here translated from the Croatian journal *Quorum*, 1987) Žižek deploys this thought specifically in relation to the Slovenian band 'Laibach' (who are at the forefront of the Neue Slowenische Kunst movement). Laibach utilise imagery of self-presentation (eg in their performances and album covers) and musical idioms and sources, which both draw directly on material from totalitarian societies, or from martial or authoritarian traditions. This 'totalitarian' aspect to Neue Slowenische Kunst clearly demands adequate interpretation, if it is to be seen as anything more than an aestheticisation of reaction. Žižek offers just such an interpretation.

Now whereas Žižek's writing in *Looking Awry* is for the most part extremely clear, his Laibach paper is more uncompromisingly 'Lacanian'. To set the scene for a critical discussion and more general development, then, I offer a short general introduction to Lacan and to the specifics of Žižek's Laibach paper in turn.

First, whilst Lacan sees himself as a psychoanalyst in the Freudian tradition, his relation to this tradition is, substantially, a revisionist one. Of decisive importance in this respect are his notions of the mirror-stage, and the acquisition and function of language. In early infancy the child's awareness is essentially scattered. Whatever consciousness it has, is a chaotic function of the gratifications which it receives from different zones and orifices of the body. However, sometime after the age of about six months, the child encounters its own image in objects which are able to mirror its appearance. The mirror-image follows patterns of symmetry and fixed variation, which, for the child suggest a unity of self and bodily co-ordination, which are, in fact, not achieved until its motor capacities are much more mature and integrated. The mirror allows the child to project an Imaginary unity of self. This projection of a 'specular ego' proves to be a decisive trait in relation to all modes of human awareness. We project fantasies of unity and completeness on to situations and phenomena which do not have such unity.

The reason why our relation to the world lacks this Imaginary dimension of unity, is bound up with our status as linguistic subjects. According to Lacan, as well as identifying with its specular ego, the child has an absolute need to receive unconditional love and recognition from its mother. It identifies itself with the supreme object of the mother's Desire, namely the phallus. However, the gratification of this identification/ desire, cannot be realised. Indeed the figure of the Father threatens castration as a penalty. However, the child is able to achieve some compensation for all this, by displacing its desire on to items which it can make present or absent at will. In this way it achieves an Imaginary control of the mother Language – with its foundations in differential relations of presence and absence (ie the fact that its units can only signify insofar as their presence is defined against a background of similar items which are *not* present) – is the best articulation of this. Language is able to express this relation to the mother, because its foundation in presence/absence follows characteristics of the object of the mother's desire, namely the phallus. This object is manifest and external but (seemingly) detachable; it can appear as erect or as flaccid; its specific modes of presence are, in other words, simultaneously inscribed with the possibility of absence. It thus embodies the relation which is the foundation of linguisticality. Indeed, Lacan regards it as the *Master* signifier which represents the field of signification as a whole.

Now the acquisition of language not only allows the child an Imaginary control of the mother's desire, but also (insofar as it has the authority of a pre-given framework into which the child is initiated) it enables the child to identify with the 'name of the Father'. On these terms, the Oedipal drama is not simply the basis of neurosis in adult life, it is a foundation of the child's entry into the symbolic order of social relations and institutions of which language itself is the supreme expression. It constitutes and stabilises the self.

However, there are several important points to note here. First, the processes described above are in essence unconscious ones. The child is not explicitly aware of the needs and desires which propel it into language. Second, the compensation which it receives through this initiation are radically transient and incomplete, but despite this are, nevertheless, insistent and recurrent. In this respect, we will recall that the child's acquisition of language – its use of signifiers – expresses (through its evocation of the phallus) a demand for absolute love and recognition from the mother. However, the mother cannot satisfy this demand, and it is displaced into linguistic life generally, as an unconscious demand for recognition from the Other. This non-adequation between need and demand – which Lacan terms 'Desire' – is endlessly perpetuated in all our linguistic transactions. Indeed, we become what we are through that demand for recognition from the Other which is implicitly involved in every expression of language. Our address to the Other is constitutive for our own self. Whatever specific objects we desire, whatever goals we formulate, whatever projects we initiate, these are given intelligibility by their meaning in relation to the overall field of other language-users. The Other, and indeed the big Other of the field of Otherness in general, is the unconscious determinant of all conscious life. However, whilst – in the grips of the Imaginary – we proceed as if our address to the Other will be adequately reciprocated – it *cannot* be. For the Other is just as split and divided as ourselves, and is unable to reciprocate our demands in any unconditional sense. It returns our demands (as Lacan puts it) in an inverse form.

The upshot of all this is that whilst the symbolic order (of language and its derivatives) enables us to articulate Otherness – be it of other people, language, or the world in general – it is shot through with transience and instability. The self is ex-centric. It involves a ceaseless generation of meaning within an overall field which it cannot control. Because we are beings whose consciousness is characterised by language, we are always 'on the way' to semantic and existential destinations which shift even as we seem to arrive there. As soon as one set of desires is realised, a new set has taken its place, and so on. We are haunted by lack, insofar as the object of desire can only be defined and appropriated against a shifting broader framework of desires in the field of Otherness, which (as noted earlier) cannot itself be fully defined and appropriated. To this complex relation between desired object and that unattainable framework of presences and absences which make it possible, Lacan gives the technical term 'objet petit *a*'. It is a kind of constant remnant or surplus which both conditions and is left over in any act of linguistic communication, and which, thereby propels us towards new acts of communication.

From this it will be gathered that the life of everyday consciousness is a ceaseless dialectic between the Sym-

bolic order, which both determines and disrupts; and the Imaginary, which involves fantasies of total realisation. The symbolic gives consciousness a fragile, transient order, whilst the Imaginary seeks to totalise this order. As Žižek observes (in *Looking Awry*, p6), 'fantasy designates the subject's "impossible" relation to a [ie objet petit *a*] the object-cause of its desire'. Indeed, 'it is precisely the role of fantasy to give the co-ordinates of the subject's desire, to specify its object, to locate the position the subject assumes in it.' In Lacanian terms, it is the task of psychoanalysis to give the subject access to a mode of speech where signification will once more become fluid, and will resist the distorting totalisations of the Imaginary and its fantasies.

There is one other feature of Lacan's overall position which must be noted. That which the Symbolic and Imaginary dimensions of consciousness give organisation to is the 'Real'. In Lacanian terms, the real is an elusive concept. We do not have any *direct* experience of it *in itself*, however, it shows through the symbolic framework at certain extreme or privileged moments. An example of the former is in psychotic delusion, where voices seem to come 'from nowhere'. Here, signifiers have broken loose from their usual metonymic and metaphoric chains and linkage, and evoke purely Imaginary presences. In this breakdown of linguistic authority, the lawlike ('name of the Father') character of language appears as an external alien power. Here the Real – that which exceeds linguisticality – shows through in a traumatic form. There are also less traumatic manifestations. One of these is a kind of 'autistic' enjoyment taken in signification for its own sake (the so-called 'sinthome' of Lacan's later work). I will return to this in some detail later on.

Given this lengthy summary of Lacan, we are now in a position to elucidate Žižek's argument in 'The Enlightenment in Laibach'. Žižek begins by considering the relation between the rational autonomy of the human subject and the exercise of this autonomy in the systematic following of rules. (For Kant, freedom in its rational sense consists in our capacity to act in accordance with our 'own idea of laws'.)

Now in Enlightenment culture and its continuing legacy, the relation between autonomy and its systematic and ha-

bitual exercise, is not fully thought through. In his earlier works, Žižek sees this as an issue of particular concern, given the rise of totalitarian ideologies. In these ideologies, the dimension of habitual obedience to law seems to actively suppress the autonomy which it is meant to articulate. Autonomy is transformed into mere autonomism; and it is the senselessness of this autonomism which is revealed by Laibach's performances.

Žižek's more recent analysis of Laibach takes a different approach – derived from the later work of Lacan. His first substantial point concerns the relation between a subject (S), the signifier by which the subject is represented (S_1) to all other signifiers (S_2). Here (as we saw in my general outline of Lacan), discourse always remains incomplete insofar as it is conditioned by a surplus or remnant – the 'objet petit *a*'. (The discourse of university knowledge attempts to deal with this remnant but only by an unrecognised repetition of the Master's discourse). What *really* interests Žižek, however, are the remaining two discourses.

The first is that of the Hysteric. Here communication is not that of the Master addressing or representing him or herself to the Other; rather it is a form of discourse which seeks out an explanation. For the Hysteric is divided between, on the one hand, his or her self-understanding at the symbolic level, and on the other hand a complex of putatively inexplicable symptoms in his or her behaviour. 'What,' asks the Hysteric of the analyst, 'is the relation between these two aspects of my being?' The origins of this problematic lie in the Hysteric's inability to achieve self-recognition as object.

The discourse of the analyst is paradoxical insofar as he or she in is effect asked to occupy a place akin to the objet petit *a* ie to identify with (and thence be able to explain) the conditions which exceed but sustain the Hysteric's symptoms. In a particularly difficult section of his argument, Žižek goes on to clarify the analyst's position here by linking it to a major point where Lacan sees the Real as breaking through the communicative network. One aspect of this concerns signification itself. In his later work Lacan holds that a key feature of signifiers is, as it were, their capacity to float. Signifiers are real material objects which, through location in specific linguistic contents, achieve specific sorts of meaning. However, their capacity to be used in this way – our sheer ability to play with or fix them – is the source of a distinctive, real enjoyment which is not socially mediated. In the final analysis, in other words, language-use embodies a dimension of enjoyment which is not simply a function of the address to the Other. It is a part of the subject's – the One's – presignifying or prediscursive being. (This enjoyment, of course, is, for the most part, assimilated into the discursive chain, fixed by the field of otherness.)

Žižek links this distinctive mode of enjoyment to Lacan's analysis of the symptom. For Lacan, a hysterical symptom is one where symbolic communication is suspended. The Hysteric cannot explain his or her symptoms. Their meaning is hidden or enciphered. It is an address to the Other, but one in which the subject fails to achieve self-recognition. It is the analyst's role to receive and interpret this address, thus reviving the communicative chain. Despite success in this, however, the symptoms persist. Why is this?

Lacan's answer is that persistence is due to the subject enjoying his or her symptoms. The discourse of the analyst deals with this through interpretations which focus on contrasting juxtapositions of symptom and fantasy. These two phenomena have different traits. In having symptoms explained, the subject finds pleasure in both the explanation and the discussions of it. On the other hand, whilst giving ourselves up to fantasy and reverie gives great enjoyment, we are loathe to explain them or offer them up to the interpretation of others. The analyst leads us from an interpretation of symptoms to an unmasking of what is ultimately at stake in the fantasies embedded in them. The subject is thus able to 'exceed' the fantasy, and be distanced from it.

The persistence of the symptom after this process is due to its embodiment of the 'sinthome'. Žižek explains this term of Lacanian art as 'the symptom in the dimension of enjoyment-of-the-real; the symptom as uninterpretable, as the direct condensation of a certain One-signifier of an external differential chain, with the object-of-the-enjoyment S_1 – a'. Here our enjoyment is in the symptom *per se*, rather than in the fantasies which

pertain to it. The subject does not seek an interpretation of the symptoms – a deciphering of them. He or she enjoys the sheer capacity for engaging in meaningful behaviour – for manipulating signifiers. This private enjoyment is an affirmation of the Real in positive terms. Rather than give up in the face of signification in all its complexity, we celebrate its generative power by identifying with one of its contingent and opaque manifestations. We thus express the *One*, the self on its way to the Other, rather than the self as constituted by the Other.

This enjoyment in exercising the capacity to signify per se, is not just one pleasure amongst others, it is a positive affirmation which is the condition of sanity itself. For if we could not take a pleasure in the capacity to signify – to make floating signifiers determinate (in whatever sense) – we would lose the basis of our systematic hold on the world. Enjoyment through the sinthome, in other words, is the ultimate expression and guarantor of consistency in human experience.

Given all this, the identification of the analysand with his or her symptoms is the final stage of the discourse of the analyst. It is paradoxical. For rather than issue in some state of general existential enlightenment concerning his or her specific relation to the world (ie an identification with the fantasy) the analyst leads the analysand to what is, in effect, an affirmation of his or her urge to deploy meaning, the urge *to be*, in its most primal sense.

It is this Lacanian strategy which defines Žižek's approach to Laibach. Laibach adopt the aesthetic trappings (or rather, aestheticise the symptoms) of numerous different aspects of totalitarian and nationalist behaviour. Their performances mix up the symptoms in a way that decontextualises their original authoritarian matrix. Rather than present a performance addressed to the Other's powers of interpretation and fantasy, they engage in a spectacle based on a scattering of the automatist symptoms of authoritarian behaviour.

Now in some cases, an identification with the symptoms is a kind of guilty reversion into madness. Using his characteristic strategy of reference to mass-culture, Žižek illustrates this by the examples of a Ruth Rendell story and a Donald Duck cartoon. In these works, the protagonists undergo a

trauma which leads to behaviour – mimicking a specific alien force – which is symptomatic of guilt. In Lacanian terms this is a case of 'acting out'. Such actions are an attempt to give symbolic expression to a meaning that is so traumatic as to resist overt symbolic articulation. The ciphered meaning of the symptoms is a reproach to the Other, wherein the subject is able to expiate his or her guilt. This must be contrasted with the 'passage to act', which rather than involve an address to the Other (ie a symbolic act), actually involves a withdrawal from the signifying network. Laibach instantiate this passage to act. For by dislocating the symptoms of authoritarian behaviour, this enables us to identify with these symptoms regarded as *sinthome*, ie as an expression of the sheer power to signify in a rule-governed way. In this manner the social bond which fixes the signifier in authoritarian context, is radically subverted. This is not a revelation of truth in the sense of correspondence with an object. Rather it is an evocation of that Real power – enjoyment of the signifier – which lies at the heart of subjectivity itself.

Without remarking upon it, Žižek, thus returns us to his starting point in relation to the Enlightenment. For the exercise and articulation of rational autonomy through the systematic following of the rules, embodies a deep-seated enjoyment of the act of signification as its condition. This is what Laibach's subversion of mere automatist rule-following points us towards.

Given this introduction to Lacan and Žižek, the reader may now scrutinise Žižek's argument in all its complexity.

Page 76: Laibach in performance

THE ENLIGHTENMENT IN LAIBACH

SLAVOJ ŽIŽEK

When Kant puts the motto of the enlightenment as not just, 'Think with your own head' but adds to this (what was at that time a disturbing but decisive continuation) 'Think as much as you want and about whatever you want, only obey!', he is rightly placed in the forefront of a new age of thought. This was first theoretically articulated by Pascal in his problematic of the relationship between mind and machine in human beings (the machine is in the highest instance 'the letter', signifying automatism). The first step of the imminent critique of the enlightenment would thus be how the 'free thinking' subject frees himself from radical dependence upon 'the letter', 'habit', 'automatism', 'machine' (the latter expression is used by both Pascal and Kant); our knowledge is proportionally externalised: its truth is determined in terms of external 'habit', which we 'automatically' follow.

The question of interest here is: is this step still satisfactory when we are confronted with 'totalitarian ideologies'? Does the 'secret' of the power of these ideologies consist in the fact that this dimension of 'obeying', the following of habit (actually concealed in the everyday life of enlightenment), openly breaks through? This question has a self-critical edge: the author of these lines himself suggested such explanations of the mechanism of 'totalitarian' ideologies (in the work 'Toward the Logic of Totalitarianism' in *History and the Unconscious*, Ljubljana, 1982). In addition to this he also offered an interpretation of the 'Laibach' phenomenon, which operates at the same level. According to this interpretation, Laibach 'alienates' the ideology which it mimics in its performances by showing its ritual as senseless automatism (from *Philosophy through Psychoanalysis*, Ljubljana 1984, pp100-29). In this text we will proceed in two ways: first, with an outline of the notional apparatus of the last and fourth stage of Lacan's reflection, which enables us to transfer the level of 'habit' (of signifying

automatism) in the direction of enjoyment-in-the-symptom. And, on that level, a new reading of the Laibach phenomenon will be offered.

Let's start with Lacan's matrix of the four discourses (from J Lacan, *Encore*, Ljubljana, 1985, p17). Its basis, the first discourse, is that of the master: a certain signifier (S_1), represents the subject (S) for another signifier, or more precisely, for all other signifiers (S_2). The problem is that this operation of signifying representation never entirely comes off without producing some disturbing surplus, 'excrement', leftover (a), and the other three discourses are three attempts to 'come to terms with', to clear up this uncomfortable remnant, the objet petit *a*.

The discourse of the university immediately takes this leftover for its object, its 'other', and tries to transform it into a 'subject' by applying knowledge to it. This is the elementary logic of the pedagogical process. We are confronted with an 'untamed' object (the 'unsocialised' child) and by means of an implantation of knowledge we try to produce a subject. The concealed, repressed truth of the discourse of the university is, thus, that behind the semblance of neutral science (which the object-pupil is related to) is hidden the gesture of the master.

The discourse of the Hysteric begins from the opposite side. Its basic constituent is a question addressed to the master: 'Why am I what you make me be?', ie, 'Why I am represented exactly by this signifier? The Hysteric is definable in terms of the experience of a fissure between the signifier that represents him (with the symbolic mandate that determines him), and the uncomfortable surplus of the object: by the split between his symbolic and his real-object-existence. He tries to produce knowledge which answers the question of how symbolic existence is founded in real object-existence, ie he seeks to abolish the split between the two exist-

OPPOSITE AND OVERLEAF: Laibach in performance

ences. This split is conditioned by the performative nature of the symbolic mandate (by the fact that statements themselves are an expression of symbolic existence). In other words, the problem of the Hysteric is his inability to recognise himself as an object. At the level of symbolic existence he asks the question, 'What is in me more than myself?'

The discourse of the analyst is exactly inverse of that of the master. The position of the analyst is defined by the fact that he occupies a place which, in the discourse of the master, plays the role of the surplus object. He identifies himself directly with the leftover of the discursive network. This is why the discourse of the analyst is far more paradoxical than it may appear at first sight. The discourse (social relation) starts to weave itself precisely from the element, which, *per definitionen*, enters the discourse – but which is also constituted as a surplus, leftover of the discourse.

A problem usually forgotten here is that, for the discourse, for the social bond, for communication, or, more precisely, for meaning with all its paradoxes (or in spite of all paradoxes that it implies), Lacan's matrix of the four discourses is actually a matrix of four possible positions in the intersubjective communicative network. Communication is, of course, structured like a paradoxical circle in which the receiver returns the sender his own message in its inverted form, ie it is the decentred Other that decides the true meaning of what we have said. (In this sense it is the S_2 that is the true master signifier conferring meaning retroactively upon S_1.) What circulates between subjects in symbolic communication is first of all lack itself, and its circulation is the condition of the exchange of positive meaning etc. But all these paradoxes are immanent to communication or meaning: the very signifier of nonsense, the signifier without a signified, is – as Lacan says – the condition of the possibility of the meaning of all the other signifiers. This means that we must never forget that the non-sense with which we are here concerned is strictly internal to the field of meaning. It truncates it 'from within'. (We did not say 'communication or meaning' without reason, because these two are ultimately the same: they coincide.) It is

always this meaning that is communicated, transmitted in the communication (even in its negative form of nonsense, of lack). At the same time the meaning is always communicative and intersubjective, ie constituted through the circulation of communication. It is not given in advance. Rather through it, the other becomes the one, who returns – who gives to the sender the real meaning of his statement.

All the effort of Lacan's last years or 'fourth phase' is directed at breaking through this field of communication aua – meaning. After he had succeeded in establishing a definitive, logically purified structure of communication/ social bond, on the basis of the matrix of the four discourses, he undertook the outline of a space where signifiers are in their 'floating' state, prior to discursive articulation, ie in a kind of space of 'pre-history', preceding the social bonding. In the seminar *Encore* an enigmatic fact is immediately indicated: the reaffirmation of the problem of the sign. The 'official' position of most of Lacan's texts from the 50s and 60s involves a shift from the sign to the signifier. In the sign we deal with a metaphysical submission of the signifier to the signified etc – the logic of the signifier outlines the autonomous signifying mechanism, which as its effect produces meaning. Why (given this) does a shift in the opposite direction – from the signifier to the sign – occur? Lacan's logic is as follows: the signifier is defined by an enclosure, which separates it from the signified and also, as the 'signifier of nonsense', it is still (although negatively) defined by its relation to the field of meaning. Lacan's effort is thus directed towards the isolation of the status of the signifying material before it is related to the field of meaning. One of the available names for this pre-signifying status of the signifying material is the sign; the other two names are the letter or, more precisely, the writing (*lettre*) and *écrit*. All three examples converge in the effort to catch the pre-symbolic object, the real status of signifying material. The sign, the letter, the *écrit*, this is – if we express this in Spinozistic terms – the signifier, defined in the modus of the real; as the object.

If the signifier is, in its symbolic mode, defined by its relation to meaning or, more precisely, its enchaining in certain social relations, and if this is the

signifier in its real mode (as object defined by its relation to enjoyment), then Lacan's word game in *Encore* when he expresses *jouissance* as 'jouissense', as enjoyment in-meaning, is clearer. The whole 'sense' of the letter or the *écrit* is in its enjoyment: the letter is signifying material as far as it does not yet produce meaning but is still, nevertheless, permeated with enjoyment. This enjoyment does not have an intersubjective nature. It is not mediated by specific social bonds, but is originally and radically 'autistic' or 'psychotic'. In such enjoyment I am my own partner, or, precisely, my partner is my body. Meaning is always the meaning of the Other, but not the enjoyment. Here we see Lacan's answer to the question why the 'letter/writing always comes to its addressee' (the last sentence of Lacan's essay on Poe's *Purloined Letter*); we usually forget (in fact to some degree Lacan himself forgot this in his first interpretation in Seminar II), that the letter in Poe's story has the status of the letter-object. It is not significant as a bearer of meaning but is at first a bearer of a certain mortal, dangerous enjoyment. And because the enjoyment is autistic and not intersubjective, it is clear why 'the letter/writing always comes to its addressee, because radically speaking its only addressee is its sender himself'.

This position clarifies another feature, which is evident even in a superficial reading of the seminar *Encore*. It is a shift homologous to that from signifier to the sign, from the Other to the One. Up to this fourth phase, all Lacan's effort was directed towards delineating a certain otherness preceding the One: first, in the field of signifier as differential, where every One is defined by a bundle of differential relations to its Other (ie every One is pre-conceived as 'one-among-the-others'). That is why the One is already isolated in the domain of the great Other (its own ex-time, its impossible-real kernel). The objet petit *a* is in a way 'the other in the midst of the Other itself', a foreign intrusion in the territory of the Other. Suddenly, in *Encore* we stumble upon a certain One (from there is One, *Y a de l'Un*) that is not one-among-the-others, that does not yet partake of the articulation of the Other. This One is, of course, precisely the One of pre-signifying enjoyment; of the signifier enchained, a freely floating element permeated with enjoyment. That is why indeed, there are more of these Ones. Hence Lacan notes: $S_1(S_1(S_1(S_1 ——S_2)))$ (*Encore*, p117).

These 'Ones before the Other' are in fact pre-communicative Ones, pre-discursive Ones, still directly permeated with enjoyment. That is why the formula is: S_1–a. The field of the great Other is constituted through 'suture', through discursive articulation of these Ones; a certain signifier which is originally S_2, ie which comes later, subsequently suspends their floating and becomes S_1, in relation to which all the others are totalised as S_2. With this we came closer to the status of the symptom in late Lacan. Symptom consists of S_1–a, the One still directly permeated with enjoyment which, as such, enters the discursive chain, fastened in the field of the Other.

Through the notion of the symptom we find the best elucidation of the path that Lacan followed from the start of his research in the 50s. At this time he understood the symptom as an opposite signifying formation, directly addressed to the Other, which gives it its real meaning. Let us follow, therefore, the complex interweavings of this.

Lacan's original position, we will recall, is that the symptom appears in the 'lack of a word', where the circulation of the symbolic communication is suspended. The symptom is 'the continuation of the communication by other means'. The hidden word is articulated as a cipher. This means that whilst the symptom is not available to immediate interpretations, it is nevertheless constituted as an address to the great Other. This great Other is always already here to offer interpretation. In the psychoanalytic situation it is the psychoanalyst who embodies the great Other, and in this situation the symptom is addressed to the analyst, in the purified self-representing state. In this respect, one might say that the symptom exceeds itself towards interpretative solution. The function of analysis, here, is the renewal of the suspended communicative chain; and when the analyst enables the analysand to name this specific meaning of the symptom, the symptom is resolved – it disappears. Here, however, problems arise. Why does the symptom in spite of successful or 'proper' interpretation, why does it not resolve; why does it persist?

Lacan's answer centres on the fact of enjoyment. The symptom is not just a ciphered message or bearer of meaning; it is, at the same time, a way in which the subject organises his enjoyment. That is why the subject, after successful interpretation, is still not ready to fully open to it. In Lacan's words, 'he loves his symptom as much as himself'. In defining this enjoyment Lacan takes two steps.

First he tries to determine the enjoyment of the symptom as a fantasy, and to oppose the symptom and the fantasy through a long series of differential moves. The symptom is a signifying formation, which circulates in its interpretation, and which can be analysed. The fantasy, in contrast, is an inert, non-analysable construct which resists interpretation or is, more precisely, addressed to the great Other which retroactively gives it meaning. Fantasy implies the crossed-out Other, ie it is placed in the empty hole in the Other. In its threatening mode, the symptom provokes a feeling of anxiety, but interpretation pleases us. We gladly explain to the other what it signifies. Its 'intersubjective recognition' is a source of intellectual pleasure. On the other hand, when we give ourselves up to fantasy (for example in everyday reverie and fancies) this gives us immense enjoyment, but nevertheless, also leads to extreme discomfort or shame. We resist telling our fantasy constructions frankly to the others etc. On this basis the two-stage logic of the psychoanalytic process itself is also articulated in relation to the. interpretation of the symptom, and the exceeding of the fantasy. At first we are confronted with the analysand's symptoms, which through interpretation, involves an advance towards the fantasy (understood as that kernel of the enjoyment where the movement of interpretation is suspended). After that we have, in a decisive moment (or more precisely, in a shift of analysis), to exceed the fantasy, to be distanced from it and understand, thereby, how the fantasy construct only masks emptiness, the lack in the Other.

But, after that, the analytical experience surprises us even more unpleasantly in relation to the condition of the analysand. He, without doubt, 'passed over the fantasy', maintained a distance towards the phantasmic frame of his symbolical reality; but the fundamental symptom still remains. How is this fact explained? What do we do with the symptom, with this pathological formation which still exists not only after interpretation but also after the fantasy is itself exceeded? Lacan tried to meet this challenge with the term 'sinthome' – a neologism which evokes a series of associations. (For example, synthetic-artificial human being, 'synthesis' of the symptom and fantasy – enjoyment, St Thomas, the saint, the saint man – do not forget that Lacan understands the saint in the position of the object of surplus, etc.) The sinthome is the symptom in the dimension of enjoyment-of-the-real; the symptom as uninterpretable, as the direct condensation of a certain One – signifier of an external differential chain, with the object-of-the-enjoyment S_1–a. What is essential here is that the object a in the sinthome does not play the role of the fantasy object. Indeed, we should not be led astray by the formula of the fantasy (S a) into believing that the only possible status of the object a is the status in the fantasy, or, more precisely, that the only possible enjoyment is enjoyment in the frame of fantasy. This would imply a horrible space, where the object would fall out of the fantasy and we would reach the level of the pulsation/drive – the 'pure state' of the death instinct, which circulates/pulsates around the emptiness in the Other. The sinthome is a way of avoiding 'going mad', or, more precisely, the means whereby we choose 'rather something (the sinthome formation) than the nothing of radical psychotic autism where the symbolic universe is falling into ruins'. Hence enjoyment-out-of-fantasy is related to a specific signifying formation, which provides minimum consistency in our being-in-the-world. The only alternative to this sinthome is 'nothing': pure autism; any kind of 'suicide', a giving up of oneself entirely to the death instinct – towards the total destruction of the symbolic universe.

All this has direct consequences in relation to defining the final moment of the psychoanalytic process. What is to be done with the sinthome, with the symptom which, even after the exceeding of the fantasy yields this 'pathological', non-analysable leftover? Lacan's last answer is: identification with the symptom; ie the final moment of the analysis is not just the exceeding of the fantasy but, at the same time, identification with the symptom as non-analysable, with this 'psychotic' point, where what was excluded from the symptom returns in the real. An example of this is found in Lacan's account of the 'symptom Joyce'.

The reference to the psychosis of Joyce in no way indicated a kind of applied psychoanalysis: what was at stake, on the contrary, was the effort to call into question the very discourse of the analyst by means of the symptom Joyce, insofar as the subject, identified with the symptom, is closed to its artifice. And perhaps there is no better end of the analysis. (JA Miller, 'Préface', in *Joyce avec Lacan*, Paris 1987, p12)

We reach the end of the psychoanalytic process when the discourse of the analyst circulates around its limit, around the point where the subject is no longer closely identified with its symptom; when his enjoyment of it can't be caught in the analyst's social bond. This would be the last Lacanian variation on the old Eastern motto 'Thou Art That', or maybe the last reading of Freud's '*wo es war, soll ich werden*': In the real of the symptom, the subject must recognise the ultimate support of his being. Where the symptom already was, in just that place, he must identify with its 'pathological' singularity. The subject, in other words, has to recognise the element that guarantees his consistency.

We can see here the distance which Lacan travelled in the last decade of his teaching. In the 60s, he still conceived the symptom as 'a way, for the subject, to weaken desire', as a compromise formation which showed that the subject did not simply persist in his desire. Access to the truth of someone's desire is possible only through the interpretative dissolution of the symptom. Generally speaking, the formula of the final moment of analysis 'exceeding the fantasy identification with the symptom' is the paradoxical reverse of what we usually consider to be an 'authentic existential position'. This can be articulated as: 'exceeding – dissolving the symptoms – identification with the fantasy'. But is not the 'authenticity' of a given subjective position defined precisely by how far we have freed ourselves from pathological 'tics' and identified with the fantasy, with our fundamental 'existential project'? In the

Laibach, Sympathy for the Devil, *LP Cover*

last Lacan, in contrast, the analysis is over when we take a distance towards the fantasy, and exactly identify with the 'pathological' singularity on which the consistency of our enjoyment depends.

So how can we, from this point of view, define the Laibach phenomenon ? What do Laibach define with the ideological complex that they 'mimic' in their performance? We can easily say that through it they practise an operation 'from the discourse to the symptom'. In everyday life ideology functions discursively; like the cement of a social bond; its elements are proportionally 'one-among-the-others'. The way of their articulation in the ideological field, the way they are 'patched together' through the reciprocal relation signifier/master which totalises them, gives them meaning. In this respect we could refer to Lacan's already classical analysis of certain ideological elements as 'floating signifiers', whose meaning is not fixed in advance, but which are the effect of the ideological articulation in which they are enchained. The basic ideological operation is then the articulation of these elements in the field. Through this articulation the elements receive meaning; at the same time they become the elements of the discourse, ie the social bond. The question that we have to put here (the question which Laibach puts in its practice) is, what are these elements before they are caught up in ideological articulation (this transition is logical, not temporal), before they are 'one-among-the-others' in a specific constituted field, ie when they still are in the state of non-articulated 'floating'? In this state they are without meaning or sense. They are bearers of a certain jouis-sense, senseless ones, permeated with enjoyment, ie S_1–a. And this is the Laibach operation: Through their spectacle they dissolve the ideological field. The ideological elements refuse to be articulated, they find themselves in an empty space, floating as an un-connected series of Ones, permeated with limited, senseless enjoyment: over here pieces of Nazism, over there pieces of Stalinism together with pieces of the Slovene national mythology, torn out of their context, scattered around in the senseless network, where everyone remains the One, without the point of suture, which could fix the meaning.

Through the Laibach spectacle, the uniqueness of two levels of the final functioning of the analytical process, of the exceeding of the fantasy and identification with the symptom, is presented to the senses – visually demonstrated. It is clear that Laibach 'exceeds the fantasy', the phantasmagorical frame on which it rests – (what we mean here is 'social-reality'). The ideological field becomes through Laibach's operation radically alienated; the effect of Laibach's spectacle is radical de-identification. They attain this through 'identification with the symptom'. This means that in one sense Laibach themselves are radically identified with the ideological elements which they perform in their senseless, limited jouis-sense.

The basic question that remains is: how is this identification different from that which we usually understand by this term, namely the typical hysterical turn into 'madness', where the only way to get rid of the element that causes the hysteria is to identify ourselves with it? To this second mode of identification with the symptom we will consider two examples: the brilliant short story by Ruth Rendell *Convolvulus Clock* and a Donald Duck cartoon. In *Convolvulus Clock* Trixie, an elderly spinster, during a visit to her friend in a countryside, steals a fine clock from the antique shop. But once she has taken it, the clock continually evokes unease and guilt. Trixie begins to read the remarks of her acquaintances as accusations and warnings based on her act of theft. When a friend once directly mentions that a similar clock has recently been stolen from the antique shop, Trixie panics, and pushes her under a tube train. She is more and more obsessed by the ticking of the clock. Unable to take it any longer, she goes into the countryside and throws the clock from a bridge into a stream, but the stream seems shallow to her. She feels that anyone glancing down from the bridge could clearly see the clock; so she enters the water, breaks up the clock and throws the broken bits all around. However, then it appears to her that the entire stream is overflowing with the clock. When an old neighbour pulls her from the water, all bleeding, bruised and wet, Trixie keeps waving her arms about like the hands of a clock and repeating: 'Tick-tock convolvulus clock'.

Absolutely identical is the logic of the cartoon in which Donald Duck comes together with a tourist group to the heart

of a primeval forest. The guide calls their attention to the beautiful view but mention at the same time to take note of a bird which lingers close by and whose habit is to spoil tourists' snapshots. In the moment when they find, with their camera, a beautiful snapshot, the bird comes flying into the frame of the picture, repeating always the same stupid refrain. When Donald Duck wants to make his first snapshot, the bird spoils it, the same happens with the next, etc. The bird avoids the rest of Donald's fellow travellers so that Donald is more and more in despair and upset, until finally he breaks down and takes to drink . . . The last scene of the cartoon: the new group of tourists is coming, the guide calls their attention to the difficult bird which spoils snapshots, and when the first tourist gets his camera ready, and is ready to press the shutter, Donald Duck duly enters the frame, moving wildly and repeating the original bird's refrain. What do we mean by 'identification with the symptom'? The gestures of Laibach signify the fact that it is possible to get rid of totalitarism, which renders us hysterical, obsesses us and drives us to despair, so that we ourselves, through reversal, identify with it; in the same way as the unfortunate Trixie herself becomes the clock and Donald Duck himself becomes the difficult bird. Here we must introduce the distinction between acting out and what Lacan calls *passage à l'acte*, passage to the act. Broadly speaking, acting out is still a symbolic act, an act addressed to the big Other, whereas a 'passage to act' suspends the dimension of the big Other, as the act is transposed into the dimension of the real. Acting out is an attempt to break through a symbolic deadlock (an impossibility of symbolisation) by means of an act even though this act still functions as the bearer of a ciphered message. Through it we attempt, in a 'crazy' way, to honour a certain debt, to wipe out a certain guilt, to embody a certain reproach to the Other. For example, the unfortunate Trixie tries through her identification with the clock to attest her innocence, to get rid of the unbearable burden of guilt. The passage to act entails in contrast an exit from the symbolic network, a dissolution of the social bond. We could say that by acting out, we identify ourselves with the symptom as Lacan conceived it in the 50s (the ciphered message addressed to the Other) whereas by passage to act we identify with the sinthome as the 'pathological form' structuring the real kernel of our enjoyment. Needless to say, Laibach's gesture is placed on this second level.

We could develop the same logic in relation to truth. In acting out, the dimension of truth still remains, and that is why the acting out is the climax of the hysterical crisis, whereas the passage to act suspends the dimension of truth and puts it on the level of the real. Basically we can define the hysterical position with the paradox of 'speaking the truth in the form of the lie or through the lie'. The hysteric at the level of literal truth (adequacy to the object) unambiguously 'lies', and through this lying, the truth of his desire, the truth of his subjective position, breaks through. Insofar as an obsessional neurosis is the 'dialect of hysteria' (Freud), we can say that what is at stake in it is the immanent reversal of this process: the obsessive 'lies in the form of truth, and through the truth'. We can recognise the obsessive in his adhering to the facts through which he tries to wipe out his subjective position. His desire to break through receives hysterical expression when he finally 'succeeds in putting it together', for example in the forced form which forges the facts.

In neurosis (hysteria and obsessional neurosis as its 'dialectic') we are always already caught in this dialectic of truth. But the 'passage to act' signifies a transition from the dimension of the truth to the enjoyment of the real. Laibach in their spectacle do not express some 'hidden truth of totalitarism'. In fact, they do not confront the totalitarian logic with its 'truth' at all. Rather they subvert it. They subvert it so that it is dissolved as an active social bond, leaving only the uneasy kernel of its limited enjoyment.

Irwin/Laibach, The Consecrated Forest, *1989, mixed media, 64x69cm*

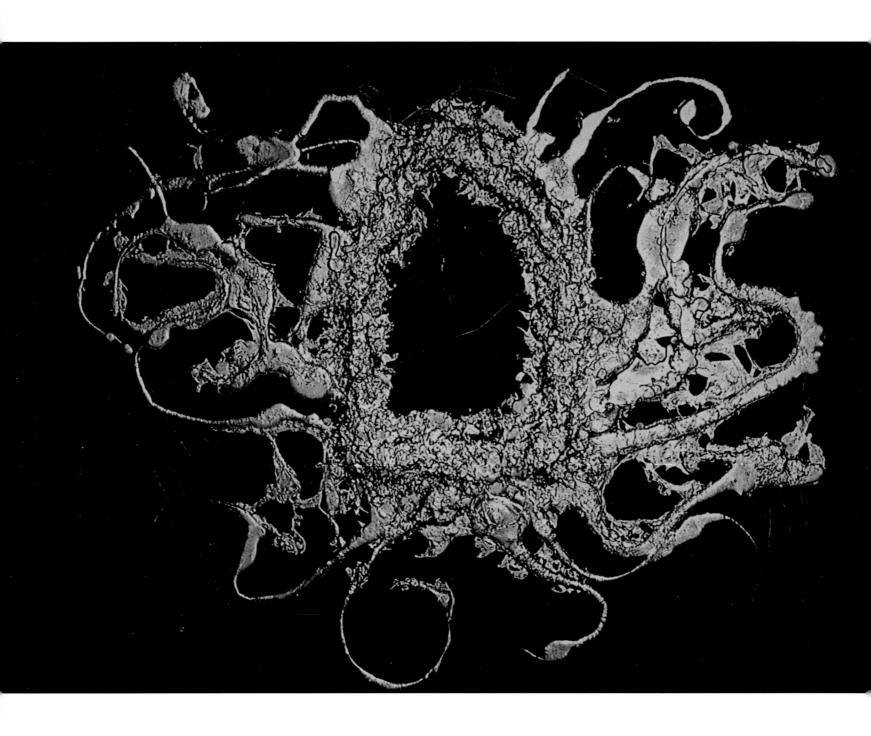

LACAN, ŽIŽEK AND THE SINTHOME

LEAVING THE 20TH CENTURY
Paul Crowther

Žižek's utilisation of Lacan in relation to Laibach is of great interest – both in itself, and in more general terms. To show this, however, demands a critical engagement with both thinkers. I shall now address this task.

First, Lacan himself. In terms of philosophical truth his relationship to Freud is of purely methodological significance in so far as Freud's psycho-analytic project is, in conceptual terms, profoundly flawed. In this respect, Lacan's use of the Freudian fairy-tale of the Oedipus complex is particularly ill-advised. For it attributes recognitional capacities to the pre-linguistic child (such as seeing the phallus as the object of the Mother's desire) which are the product of advanced linguistic experience. Matters are made even more incoherent, of course, by the fact that Lacan actually seeks to explain the child's *initiation* into language itself, in terms of the Oedipus complex.

Now if the Freudian myths are extracted from Lacan, it might seem at first sight that little remains. Certainly such notions as Lacan's technical sense of Desire, and the privileged status of the phallus must be abandoned. The one key quasi-Freudian idea which can remain is that of the unconscious per se. This idea retains its significance precisely because Lacan uses it differently from Freud, by relating it to insights drawn from Saussure and Hegel. These insights are (respectively) the notion of language and meaning as having differential structure, and the idea of the self as constituted by reference to the desire of the Other. This yields the following overall picture of the relation between subject and world.

Initiation into the symbolic order of language enables the subject to articulate its relation to the world and other people – Otherness in the broadest sense. This articulation, however, cannot be absolutely fixed. The symbolic order of language and social bonding – is a differential structure into which the subject is inserted. This means that it is the Other which fundamentally determines the meaning and content of communication, in a field of continuous semantic generation. Meaning is not simply a correspondence between the subject's private space and some clearly definable and self-contained state of affairs. Whatever one thinks or desires is determined by relations to the shifting and complex field of Otherness (things, meaning, and desire, in a global sense). There is always more to our conscious-ness of self and Other than can be articulated in any act of communication.

Now this field of Otherness in relation to which the individual achieves self-definition is fundamentally an uncon-scious matrix. Our capacity for the Imaginary, in particular, serves to affirm this. The Imaginary covers over the complex differential structures of our relation to Otherness by colonising them with fantasies of total comprehension and self-containment. We imagine the self is simply a unity which signifies directly to other unities and which sets clearly definable and realisable goals for itself. It is the task of analysis to break the rigidity of this artificial framework with a use of language which can evoke something of the complexity and contin-gency of our inherence in the Other.

Viewed in these non-Freudian terms, Lacan's strategies and concepts now appear in a more viable philosophical form as a radical existentialisation of Hegel. In particular, the Real now appears in its true role – as the sheer excess and contingency of being, upon which language allows us a hold, but only a partial and precarious one. In fact, this is the key advance of Lacan over Hegel. He gives contingency its due, as a decisive and constitutive element in the conditioning and organisation of human experience.

Given this restatement of Lacan, the vital significance of Žižek's Laibach paper lies in the emphasis which he rightly assigns to the sinthome – that

VSSD, Edges of Medusa, *1987, aluminium, paint*

89

form or 'symptom' which manifests your enjoyment of the capacity to use signifiers. This notion has a supreme philosophical significance. For it suggests that the very capacity to order the world in rational terms has a necessary connection with pleasure. Neither Lacan nor Žižek develop this beyond the level of a brute affirmation of the self in a real mode. However, the sinthome can be developed much further in terms of both its general and particular significance.

To see why this is so, let us first consider the use which Žižek makes of it in relation to the notion of the symptom. Clearly Žižek understands symptom in a much broader sense than that of the Hysterical behaviour as such. He treats symptoms as manifestations of automatist behaviour, ie habitual rule-following whose origins and structure are forgotten or unquestioned, or both. (This, of course, is a perfect characterisation of the regimentation of behaviour in totalitarian or authoritarian societies.) Now in the spectacle presented by Laibach (and, indeed, other NSK manifestations – such as the Irwin group's visual imagery) automatist symptoms are no longer fixed in the social bonds of an authoritarian society. Rather they are, as it were, brought into collision with one another. We are thus able to identify with them for their own sake, as sinthome – a mute expression of the enjoyment of signification itself.

However, what Žižek does not explicitly address is the nature of the relation which holds between identifying with symptoms, and identifying with the symptoms through *spectacle*. One presumes, for example, that one can find one's own sinthome through the acceptance of the behavioural traits which make one what one is; or (by proxy) through identifying with similar traits in others. But surely this is not the same experience as identifying with a representation of symptoms, as is found, for example, in the performances and artifacts of NSK.

Interestingly, Žižek himself points us in the right direction for dealing with this general issue, through his many analyses of film. In *Looking Awry,* Žižek suggests how some formal cinematic devices suspend external reality. In David Lynch's *Elephant Man,* for example, we find 'a series of shots that are, from the standpoint of realistic narration, totally redundant and incomprehensible,

ie the sole function of which is to visualise the pulse of the real' (p41). Indeed, these shots are the basis of the film's 'poetic beauty'. Given this we might justifiably extend Žižek's insights in the following way.

In the field of artistic production, many representations simply function as vehicles of fantasy addressed to the Other. However, when a work is stylistically original in respect of some innovation in relation to customary treatments of form and/or content, our reception of it is altered. In such cases, we enjoy the artist's style – his or her way of articulating the significatory possibilities of the medium. Now, in the foregoing example, Žižek himself links formal devices which have no realistic narrative function, to a visualisation of the 'pulse of the real'. However, this visualisation (understanding the term in a broad metaphorical sense) is also achieved when artistic form as such arrests us in the way just described. For we attend to and explore the interplay of form and content *for their own sake.* Our capacities for – in Kantian terms – understanding and imagination are brought into heightened reciprocity. What makes this so important is that it is the cooperation of these capacities which are the necessary condition of our ability to communicate – to engage in signifying activity. Now in the crudest forms of aesthetic enjoyment this cognitive exploration focuses on the relation between parts and whole in a formal configuration per se. However, in the artwork matters are different. Here we know that the configuration was created by a fellow human being. This means that it was produced by contingent activity, ie which could have gone in other directions than those which it actually did. Hence the parts of an artwork are moments of contingency when the signifying process reaches a certain stage, in transit to another stage. However, from the viewpoint of the end-product, these contingent moments are now necessary. Change any of them, and the identity of the whole is changed. Here, the artist's symptoms – his or her stylistic traits – are read in terms of their capacity to generate specific meaning from contingency. Our aesthetic enjoyment of the artistic whole, in other words, is (over and above more complex levels of significance) an enjoyment of the capacity to signify – to make the floating signifier determinate. Art itself,

VSSD, Total Ambience, *1986, mixed media installation*

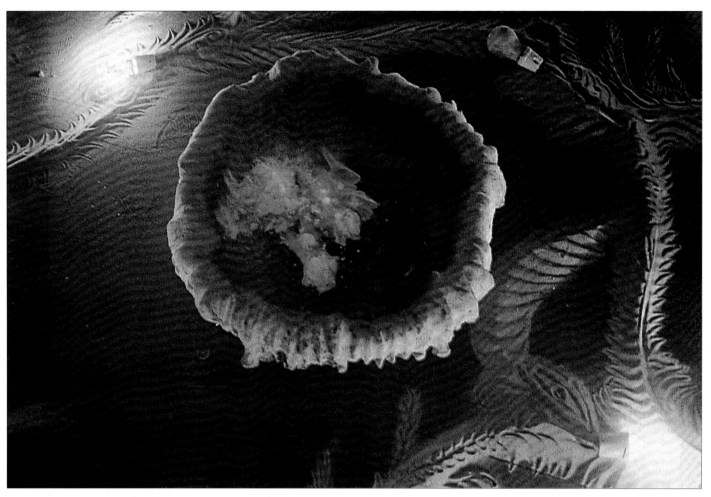

in other words, is an embodiment of sinthome.

On these terms, in other words, Žižek's discussion of Laibach is itself symptomatic of a more general significance for the sinthome. The aesthetic experience of art (or at least one of its aspects) returns us to the self in its fundamental reality. The reason why this link has not been fully developed by Žižek (or, indeed, Lacan himself) is because the aesthetic functions as an object of discourse in the Symbolic domain. It can be cultivated; and is thence assimilated within the social bond. However, even in this respect Žižek and Lacan suggest indirectly how the aesthetic might have a privileged status. The reason for this is Žižek's notion of the 'rendering of the real'. This develops a tendency in Lacan's later work to affirm the continuity of signification with the real. In this respect, Žižek suggests that

> The ambiguity of the Lacanian real is not merely a nonsymbolised kernel that makes a sudden appearance in the form of traumatic 'returns'. The real is at the same time contained in the very symbolic form: the real is *immediately* rendered by this form. (*Looking Awry*, p39).

Now whilst Žižek himself develops this in some odd directions, it relates more immediately to points which I made earlier concerning art. There is a whole culture of discourse based on the production and reception of art. Aesthetic concerns – as opposed to private interests and pleasures – can be tested, developed, and revised on the basis of critical exchange and argument. However, in the final analysis all this is empty talk, unless it constantly returns to and gravitates around direct perceptual intercourse with the artwork itself. We cannot seriously consider critical verdicts which are based on only second-hand acquaintance with the objects of the verdicts. The aesthetic experience of art is rooted in the concrete particular. For it focuses on the specific way in which the artist – through the process of production – fixes signifiers, and produces meaning. The symptoms embodied in the work show this surge into meaning, in the stylistic totality of their phenomenal fabric. What this amounts to is that the irreducible sensible particularity of the artwork is not only a sinthome with which we can identify, but also

exemplifies and discloses *the rendering of the real itself*. All human artifice and activity has this significance, but only art fulfils it; for the whole culture of the production and appreciation of art is, in effect, a discourse which returns to our pleasure in the generation of meaning, as its *raison d'être*. In art the sinthome retains its affirmatory status, but in an intersubjective mode, as a constant rebirth of the symbolic order.

This is the general significance of the Lacanian sinthome. It also has a more specific (but crucial) import, which again Žižek sets the scene for, but does not develop. In this respect the particular form of the Laibach sinthome is in its presentation of automatist symptoms of totalitarianism, out of the social contexts which gives them their oppressive significance. Now, at first sight, it might seem that Laibach and NSK are *simply* a particular case of artistic sinthome. However, there is rather more to it than this, in that the automatist rule following which Laibach and NSK present, is of a particularly rigid sort. Here human behaviour identifies with a specific product of its own artifice – namely the machine. But again, there is more to it than just that. In a sense the function of all art is to externalise the self so as to be able to identify with – find oneself again – in the product. What NSK in effect does (in the most general sense) is to externalise and identify with a mode of artifice which has already (as Heidegger and many others have rightly argued) colonised the human sensibility. NSK, in other words, represent the impulse for humanity to merge with its own artifacts.

This impulse is not new; it is, in fact one of the definitive trajectories of 20th-century modernist art. The first glimmerings of it are to be found in the Cubism of Braque and Picasso, where the pictorial enterprise is re-launched in a way that tends to collapse the distinction between content, medium and the artist. As Braque noted:

> When the fragmentation of objects took place in my painting around 1910, it was as a means to getting closer to the object within the limits tolerated by the painting.

In addition to this the entire Futurist oeuvre, is, of course, a kind of wild celebration of a similar desire in relation to the machine and its effects. There is also a strong element of this in

VSSD, Total Ambience, 1986, mixed media installation

Malevich's notion of the 'economic'. Other tendencies represent fantasies of merging with rather different emphases. In Pop Art, for example, the distinction between personal expression and consumption of images and techniques from mass culture is erased; in Surrealism a whole series of oppositions (most significantly that between 'perception and representation') is seen as overcome by Surrealist practice.

Now, of course, this impulse to merge the human sensibility with the products of its own artifice, is not fully worked out in any of the tendencies just noted; and it always exists alongside other more specific and consciously formulated aims. But it is a distinct tendency, and exemplifies art's capacity to look ahead, and indeed to mediate the future. Laibach and Neue Slowenische Kunst are in this respect acutely symptomatic. Lacking a distinctive modernist tradition, the Slovenians have attempted to deal with this by an eclectic usage of imagery from those totalitarian societies who have historically been their oppressors. In so doing, they have not only thematically embodied the sinthome (which is essential to art per se) but indeed their particular articulation of it is one that actually feeds upon and declares one of the deepest impulses of modernism itself. However, in the eclecticism and diversity of their artistic means, Neue Slowenische Kunst give this a distinctive contemporary voice, and point towards its on-going *postmodern* significance.

Interestingly, the most significant new development of this impulse is found in another Slovenian art group, namely VSSD. Their work employs imagery which suggests the systematic interchangeability of the technological and the organic. Consider, for example, the installation *The Red Sea (The Red Planet)*. Of itself the title sets up associations of both the organic world and space exploration. In physical terms, the scattered visual components deployed by the artist do not declare the existing space of the site, neither do they subvert it. Rather they colonise it in a positive way. The diversity of materials and objects used – as well as their quantity – create a sense of repetition and overload. Yet there is a sense of system here. Not that of scientific law in its conventional modes, but rather of direction-within-contingency ie the world of fractals, and computer simulation.

What is at stake here is an aesthetic of systematicity as such, wherein the sensibility finds itself at home in, and expressed by, the structure and *aura* of its own technological artifice.

Now whilst the impulse to identify and merge with the products of artifice is a recurrent trajectory in modern and postmodern art, VSSD invoke this in its highest stage. They exemplify the origins of a new sensibility wherein the organic and technoscientific are totally integrated. The culminating of this will be a *physical* merging of the human organism with its artifacts, and the engendering of new models of signification, and indeed of rationality as such. Baudrillard's notion of the hyperreal is a vague foretelling of this, but does not take account of how our embodied condition resists the assimilation of reality and its simulacra. However, this day of assimilation will come. Suppose, for example, that our capacity to recall the past and imagine the future could be synthesised in exact virtual terms through suitable biomechanical implants. We would still be finite beings, but the existential structure of finitude – our relation to both ourselves and Otherness – would be radically transformed. The scope of the Imaginary would be diminished in some respects and augmented in others. In such a situation the basis of consistency in experience, would *not* be our sheer capacity to achieve signification and to identify with the contingent symptoms which exemplify this. Rather it would consist in our capacity for projecting and deploying alternative systems for configuring our relation to the world. Our pleasure in the sinthome, in other words, would be transformed. It would consist in the enjoyment of positing alternative modes of signification; of identifying with the contingency of symptoms per se.

Of course these possibilities are hard to comprehend in anything other than the most schematic terms. This is because they mark a point where the human species would evolve into a different order of being. This outcome of our discussion should hardly be surprising. For the growth of modernity has brought with it visions of a future man – sometimes Utopian, sometimes apocalyptic, but always in effect simply *Homo sapiens* in new contexts. However, the deeper ramifications of modernism's technoscientific innovations have always pointed in the evolutionary directions just alluded to. But within the constraints of rationality as it exists at present, it is almost impossible to articulate what other possibilities of rationality are like. However, they can at least be evoked or suggested in terms of the various alternative modes of representation (using the representation in the very broadest sense) which have been opened up by tendencies within both modern and postmodern art.

I shall end with two observations. First, there are, I think, much better philosophical models than Lacan's for articulating the present nature of our embodied relation to the world. However, the merit of his thought – if stripped of its Freudian baggage – is that it gives proper due to the role of signification, contingency, and Otherness in human experience. In fact, even if the structure of finitude is, in time, transformed (in the ways noted above), these notions, and indeed the Lacanian Real, will still be key players in the drama. Indeed, it may be that his thought is flexible enough to articulate continuity and difference between *Homo sapiens* and its evolutionary Other.

This brings me to my second observation. Following Lacan and Zizek, I have assigned central importance to the notion of the sinthome in experience as it is currently constituted. I have also tried to show that it has a vital relation to art and the aesthetic. It is a constant around which these modes of practice and receptivity (in part) gravitate. This constant, however, is mediated by the different historical modes of such practice and receptivity. This mediation is not just a matter internal to the field of art. Rather it can be inaugurated by and point towards much broader dimensions of human experience. The fact that I have focused on Neue Slowenische Kunst and VSSD is symptomatic of this. At the end of the 20th century we have experienced a postmodern sensibility characterised by unabashed eclecticism. Much of this is empty and directionless, and more so in the late 1980s and 1990s. However, by virtue of both historical and geographical contingencies, NSK and VSSD have been able to give the contemporary eclectic garb of the sinthome quite distinctive expression. In so doing, the former movement exemplifies a continuity between modernity and postmodernity; whilst the latter duo point towards a radical future transformation of the sinthome – in the next century and beyond . . . Thus are constants historically mediated.

LEFT AND OVERLEAF: VSSD, The Red Sea (The Red Planet), *1991, mixed media*

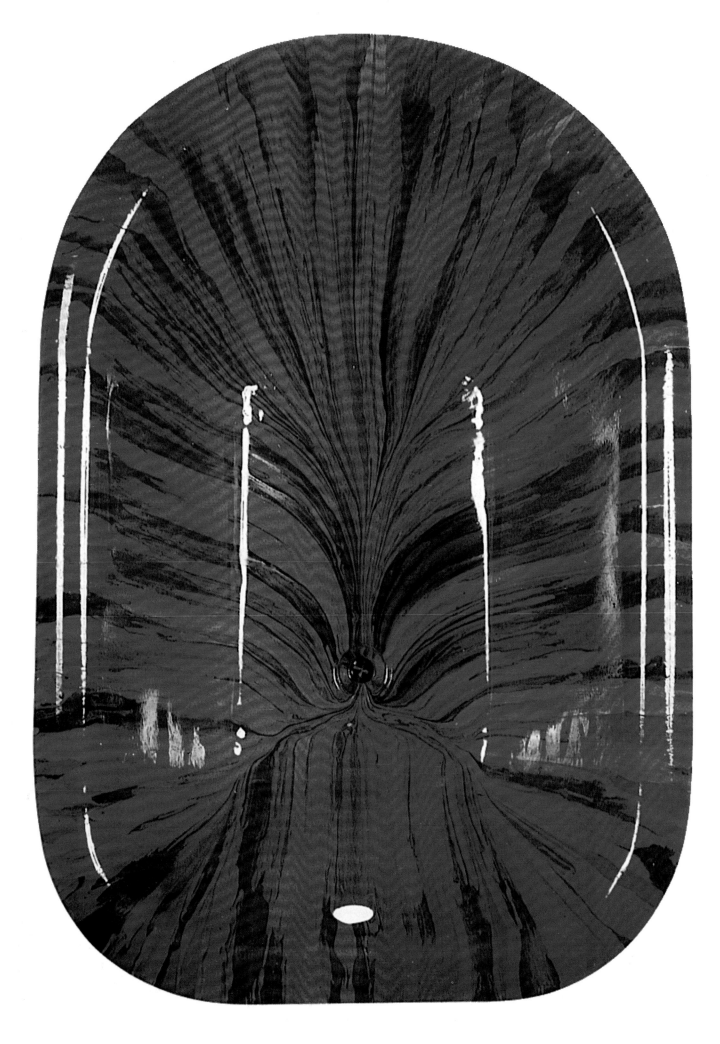